The Group as Therapist

The International Library of Group Analysis

Series Editor: Malcolm Pines

The aim of this series is to represent innovative work in group psychotherapy, particularly but not exclusively group analysis. Group analysis, taught and practised widely in Europe, has developed from the work of S.H. Foulkes.

of related interest

Circular Reflections
Selected Papers on Group Analysis and Psychoanalysis
Malcolm Pines
International Library of Group Analysis 1
ISBN 1 85302 492 9 pb
ISBN 1 85302 493 7 hb

Group Psychotherapy of the Psychoses
Concepts, Interventions and Context
Edited by Victor L. Schermer and Malcolm Pines
ISBN 1 85302 584 4 pb
ISBN 1 85302 583 6 hb

Taking the Group Seriously
Towards a Post-Foulkesian Group-Analytic Theory
Farhad Dalal
International Library of Group Analysis 5
ISBN 1 85302 642 5 pb

The Psyche and the Social World
Developments in Group-Analytic Theory
Edited by Dennis Brown and Louis Zinkin
International Library of Group Analysis 17
ISBN 1 85302 928 9 pb

INTERNATIONAL LIBRARY OF GROUP ANALYSIS 14

The Group as Therapist

Rachael Chazan

Forewords by Pat de Maré
and Malcolm Pines

Jessica Kingsley Publishers
London and Philadelphia

The extract form W.W. Gibson's poem on page 92 is reproduced with the kind permision of Palgrave Publishers Ltd.

First published in the United Kingdom in 2001 by
Jessica Kingsley Publishers Ltd
116 Pentonville Road
London N1 9JB, England
and
325 Chestnut Street
Philadelphia, PA 19106, USA

www.jkp.com

Library of Congress Cataloging in Publication Data
A CIP catalogue record for this book is available from the Library of Congress

British Library Cataloguing in Publication Data
A CIP catalogue record for this book is available from the British Library

ISBN 1 85302 906 8

Printed and Bound in Great Britain by
Athenaeum Press, Gateshead, Tyne and Wear

Contents

Part 1 Perspectives on Group Analytic Therapy

Part 2 Special Kinds of Groups

Part 3 Ethics and the Group

For Michael
who made it all possible

Acknowledgements

This book took shape in my head over many years, and I am grateful to all those who encouraged me in working with groups and breaking new ground. My thanks to Drs Alan Edwards and Bruin Tammes, whose groups on the neurosis unit at Napsbury, near London, England, I observed, and to Dr R.D. Scott, who, at the same hospital, taught me much about psychotherapy with schizophrenics. Particular thanks are due to Dr Julia Erenfeld, who, as acting medical director of Kfar Shaul Hospital, Jerusalem, gave me *carte blanche* to turn my admission ward into a therapeutic community, and to work with patients as well as families in groups. My thanks to Dr S. Litman, who permitted me to pioneer a group with post-psychotic outpatients, which became a model for others, and Dr E. Danilowitz, who encouraged the continuance of this venture. I am grateful to all my co-therapists: the late Immanuel Cohen, who partnered me in my first couples groups, helping to shape concepts and practice; and my subsequent partner, Moshe Krupnik. My very open-minded co-therapists in the outpatient group with psychotic patients included Noah Rotem, Marcia Levene-Shvira and Naomi Paynton; in the neurotics/borderline group Margalit Jacob was my co-therapist for a time.

My special thanks to Geoffrey Elkan, clinical psychologist, who read the whole manuscript chapter by chapter, making detailed critical suggestions. I am grateful to Patrick de Maré, from whose median groups I learnt much, and who also read my manuscript, returning it with several pages of constructive criticism. I owe much to the late Charles Rycroft, my supervisor and mentor, who also read the first chapter. I am grateful to Malcolm Pines, for his unflagging encouragement in the final stages of writing and the process of publication. Last but not least, I thank my husband, Michael, for his long-standing support and encouragement in the venture of writing the book.

Rachael Chazan

Foreword

I feel honoured in having been invited by Rachael to write a foreword to her book *The Group as Therapist*. This is an extremely thoughtful and comprehensive overview, as applied contemporaneously to the present day. She does not simply give us a synopsis of the Foulkesian approach but adds her own observations: for instance, to Foulkes' comment that the group conductor's role involves bowing to the authority of the group, which in a sense idealizes the group, she points out that it is a good thing also to understand the various perspectives, including that of the group conductor himself. Rachael reminds us that everyone has to learn for themselves how to take a group. She branches out from the original Foulkesian model to group functioning from several other perspectives, e.g. groups with psychotic and borderline personalities, multiple family therapy groups, therapeutic community groups, couples groups, median and large groups as well as the peer groups of children. She writes a very significant chapter on ethical relating, holding that we cannot simply rely on the benefits of scientific and technological advance as self-evident. She holds that moral philosophy plays an undeniable role in the effective functioning of group therapy and that moral and political growth can take place as a healing process 'within the larger group of humanity as a whole'. I was intrigued by her suggestion that we have gone further than Kant in introducing empathy, reciprocity and love in place of his listed codes of duty.

This is a brilliant exposition written in a deceptively simple and readable style. It is a must!

Congratulations, Rachael: I am favoured by our friendly association over the past twenty-seven years.

Pat B. de Maré FRC Psych
April 2000

Foreword

Rachael Chazan opens her text with a question 'Why Group Psychotherapy?' Similarly, the reader will ask: 'Why another book on group psychotherapy?' The answer will emerge after reading this illuminating text.

Rachael Chazan, psychiatrist, philosopher, musician, folk dancer, interweaves her clear exposition of group-analytic theory with many clinical vignettes from her extensive experience in small, median and large groups, and therapeutic community. She is a 'broad band' therapist: she describes couples groups, multi-family groups, groups with psychotic patients. Few therapists have such extensive experiences and few have the capacity to write clearly and concisely as does our author. I was struck by the phrase, in her discussion of group cohesion: 'when cohesion becomes enmeshment and stability becomes inflexibility, a price is paid'.

Rachael Chazan works in Israel and speaks for a generation that has believed in an egalitarian democracy of Kibbutz. Throughout the book she emphasizes therapeutic factors of equality, fairness, sympathy and empathy, inherent in a Foulkesian approach.

In recent years our literature has been enhanced by authors who, appreciative of Foulkes, also point to his areas of weakness. This book is a salutary reminder of the strength of the basic model when it is applied clearly and sensitively. I felt that I was getting to know a therapist whom I would trust for myself and those close to me.

Rachael Chazan and Ronald Sandison, to whose book I have also contributed a foreword, are fine exemplars of group analysis, who acknowledge with gratitude the humanizing power of the group-analytic group as set out by Foulkes and further enhanced by Patrick de Maré.

The final chapter of this book, which sketches the relation between group therapy and economics, on moral and ethical issues, opens a window on what will further occupy us in the new millennium. Economic rivalry, competition, the struggle for the limited supply of 'positional goods', contrasts with the availability of 'relational goods', benefits that we can bestow on others and upon ourselves when we display sympathy, empathy, fairness and reciprocity. Foulkes showed us the inherent capacity of the well-selected and conducted group to move towards social and democratic norms. Today we can reinforce this view with the striking findings of evolutionary psychology. Frans deWaal (1996) has shown that primate societies (chimpanzees) manage their group relations on the basis of a genetic endowment that enabled the animals to show sympathy, to get along together and to negotiate conflicts peacefully. Virtue, defined as 'pro-social' tendencies and behaviours, is our birthright: sadly, our birthrights can be denied us by the actions of rigid bureaucracies, totalitarian regimes, life-hating tyrants. But slowly group-analytic ideas and methods are contributing to the humanizing of psychiatry and to the great good of civil society. This book is a contribution to that process.

Malcolm Pines
September 2000

Introduction

Why Group Psychotherapy?

Throughout my professional life I have been impressed by the power and fascination of groups, both as a group conductor and, at various stages, as a group member. Right at the beginning of my professional career, I sat in as an observer of a daily ward group, five days a week, for six weeks. I found it very impressive. The group was expected to do the work of treating the individual, and it appeared to do this adequately. It was the sole treatment tool on the unit; there was neither individual therapy nor pharmacotherapy. Interpretations by the two therapists were sparing, they seemed to let the group do its own work. A session might pass without their saying anything at all. It was a group-centred group, a group-analytic group in the spirit of Foulkes – though at the time I would not have been able to classify it as such.

When my post expired I applied for another in the same hospital. I was anxious about this. In the week of the interview, I was still observing the group. A man who was a patient on the unit described his feelings about a job interview he had gone through. I felt as if I were myself in therapy: this taught me about vicarious therapy in the group. A silent group member may nonetheless be doing work.

Many years later (1983–4), I took part in Pat de Maré's median group, which was for both trainees and 'patients'. It took me months to discover who belonged to which category. This may have been because all were therapists and all were patients.

Throughout my career I have used groups, sometimes introducing them into settings where there had been none. I found them powerful, in many cases clearly doing more for specific patients than individual therapy had done.

This is my personal experience; it is, of course, neither new nor unique. Group psychotherapy is being practised, in various forms, all over the world. There is a body of literature, much of it excellent. The power of the group is known and acknowledged: for example, the success of group work in the therapeutic community in helping persons with character disorder is well documented. Nothing else works as effectively.

However, there are still those who regard group psychotherapy as inferior to individual therapy. Potential clients may fear that they will receive only a small share of the therapist's attention. Professionals are by no means free from prejudice. In a psychodynamically oriented clinic in Jerusalem, there was a problem with referrals to groups. Individual therapy was tacitly assumed to be the ideal: joining a group might just shorten the waiting period. To give an example from the literature, Kymissis (1993), writing on indications for group therapy with adolescents, 'those for whom individual therapy is at an impasse, those who have problems with authority and cannot start individual therapy, and those who are financially unable to afford other types of treatment' (Kymissis 1993, p.581).

I believe, however, that the experience of group analysis is relevant and valuable not only for troubled and needy persons, but for all of us. It is important that we learn to see ourselves in the context of the group – not in the societal context, which is a game with learnable rules, but in the give-and-take that evolves in an experiential group where all members are of equal status. We have advanced in technology, in pursuing specific aims in every scientific domain, yet are extraordinarily helpless in the field of human relations, particularly group relations and social organization. Van Bertalanffy (1968, p.91) gives a simple example: in air travel, we find ourselves crossing the Atlantic at great speed, yet 'having to spend endless hours waiting, queuing, being herded in airports'. We have a highly developed technology of communication – telephones, fax, email, satellites – but in the content, the mode of communication with other human beings, our knowledge is in its infancy. We do not know how to listen, to understand one another. Conflict resolution is a relatively young discipline: in fact, we often fail at it dismally. Violence then comes to replace language.

Part of the problem is the competitive assumption: our gain must be the loss of another (cf. Hobbes 1968 [1651]). If we listen to the 'rival' or the 'adversary', we are on the way to making concessions, therefore losing out.

In our failure to think of ourselves as a group, we use our knowledge and resources in ways that are not only wasteful, but also destructive. As Fritjof Capra (1983) points out, we have been stockpiling nuclear weapons sufficiently to destroy the world many times over. In 1978 world military spending was US$425 billion per year. At the same time, more than 15 million people (most of them children) were dying of starvation each year.

We spend tremendous resources on weapons of 'defence', which are in most cases merely means of counter-aggression, unable to protect our citizens. Yet it is clear that we cannot blow up a nearby country, or any country, for that matter, without exposing ourselves to deadly fall-out. We cannot make a hole under our neighbour's seat without sinking the whole ship. We have yet to learn the most effective mode of defence – effective dialogue.

A therapeutic group is not about conforming, being all alike. It is, however, about symmetry, everyone being equally important. Foulkes (1948) held that the group effectively treats the individual, since one's individuality expresses itself in the context of others. De Maré, who worked with Foulkes, held that in the larger group, the individual treats the group. It serves to civilize society. The hate which naturally arises in large groups is transformed, slowly, by dialogue, into a form of brotherly love that he called 'koinonia' (De Maré, Piper and Thompson 1991).

We need, therefore, not only to get together in groups, but also to understand how they work, how to convene them and allow them to do their work, without power play or domination. I hope, in this book, to contribute my own small part to this endeavour; to present a model for understanding the group-analytic group, and its various applications.

Note

I have used the male and female pronouns interchangeably throughout the book.

PART 1

Perspectives on Group Analytic Therapy

CHAPTER 1

A View of Psychotherapy

How does psychotherapy work? Many theories have been put forward; perhaps all have some truth in them, psychotherapy being complex and multifaceted. I suggest that at least two things occur: psychotherapy aims to effect some change in the way that the person perceive himself and others. A relationship system is set up specifically for the purpose of therapy.

The importance of the group

The important discovery of psychoanalysis was that a person is the product of his early influences. His present behaviour is determined by what happened to him in early infancy. We might call this vertical causation. More recently, the importance of what we might call 'horizontal causation' in the interpersonal space was discovered.

Rycroft (1966, pp.10–11) points out that it is not enough to trace a symptom to a cause in the patient's past history. He writes: 'Symptoms are not an entirely individual matter – they have a social nexus and function and change in one person may be contingent on changes in others.' The patient's wish to lose symptoms has to be 'greater than his [sic] wish to retain the status quo in his personal relationships.' And, of course, the significant other, the family member, has to be interested in the change.

Each person plays a role in, and is influenced by, the transactions of the family group (and, in fact, the wider social group in which he lives). It is significant to hear the above from a psychoanalyst who was in no way involved in family therapy or the movement towards it. The concept of 'horizontal causation' plays an important part in systems theory, on which a school of family therapy is based.

One of the characteristics of horizontal causation is that it is not one-way, but circular. The behaviour of a family may 'cause' a child to behave in a certain way, and the child may 'cause' the family to respond in a certain way. Partner A may dominate partner B because B is rather weak and indecisive. Yet the fact that A is dominating may make B more afraid and more indecisive.

The issue of causation within the social group is more complex. When a child starts school, his behaviour may change. He may take on or be cast in the role of troublemaker or victim, for reasons dependent not on him alone. When a terrorist plants a bomb to kill a number of people, do we look to his childhood to explain his action? Is he violent because he experienced violence in childhood? Or do we explain his action by the dynamics of the group to which he belongs, which is perhaps an oppressed minority or, conversely, a right-wing fascist one? And, again, what is there about him that lets the group choose him to play this part?

There is no simple answer, and there cannot be. Group dynamics are complex, and cannot be ignored. One of our assumptions is that the dynamics of therapeutic (or didactic) groups in some way reflect the dynamics of groups in life.

Relationship systems in life and in psychotherapy

At one time, the individual was considered to be a self-contained unit. As far as psychotherapy was concerned, we thought we need study only the individual, and treat the individual. Psychoanalysis admitted the importance of the mother–infant relationship. It also described 'internal objects', the representation of others within ourselves. However, the impact of interpersonal relations on the individual has come to be appreciated only gradually.

Man lives in groups. It is society that enables an infant to grow into a human being. Sprott (1958) describes two girls. Anna was confined to a room and given only enough food to keep alive. She could not talk, walk or do anything that showed intelligence when found at the age of 6. Isabelle had been shut up with her deaf-and-dumb mother and was at first believed to be deaf too. After expert guidance, she was eventually able to attend a normal school. The 'wild boy of Aveyron', found among animals about 1800, was himself like an animal when discovered by a doctor. He adapted himself to human beings, but scarcely learnt to talk.

As to living in groups, the family is the most powerful of these. It does more than mould the infant's personality; it is a continuing influence. We understand now that there are subtle and reciprocal influences in groups of people that live and act closely together, particularly families. At one time, a 'problem child' might have been treated in isolation. Today it is widely realized that the 'problem' has to be understood in the context of family relationships. For example, an intelligent child who is doing badly at school might thereby be conveying a message to the family: he is in some kind of distress. A teenager refusing to eat may unconsciously be attempting to hold his parents' marriage together. Worrying about his anorexia, they become united over at least one issue.

There are important systems other than the family. The peer group is one whose power is often underestimated. Piaget (1932) describes research that shows its role in the moral development of the child.

Other systems include work organizations, the army, which is a powerful system with its own laws, the system of the psychiatric hospital, including staff and patients. Large systems of this nature are extremely complex. Let us consider families.

> Ex. 1(i). Lily Pincus (1976) describes a 10-year-old girl who climbed the highest trees, jumped from the steepest banks and constantly endangered herself. Two years of therapy made no difference. The parents were therefore invited to come into therapy; they were a charming and devoted couple. The father held a job which seemed below his potential. He explained that it was his first job; he had not left it since he could not, as a family man, afford to take risks. He had met his wife while still a student; they had waited for twelve years to marry to ensure he could offer her a good enough home. As she had a difficult pregnancy and labour, she was told to avoid further pregnancies. The couple would take no risks and refrained from further sexual relations.

> As Pincus (1976) points out, 'all the risk-taking and excitement of adventure, which these parents had denied themselves, were projected on to their only child, who, as we saw, acted it out.' After going through therapy the couple were enabled to take more risks, and their daughter no longer had to do it for them.

Davidson (1993) gives many instances of unwitting and unconscious transmission of feelings of Holocaust survivors to their children.

> Ex. 1(ii). A 16-year-old girl attempted suicide. The mother, a Holocaust survivor, admitted that she did not want to live. 'But all my life I wanted my children to be happy and my greatest failure is that, despite this, I have succeeded in transferring to them the feeling that there is no point in living.'

> Ex. 1(iii). Another girl, aged 17, was anorexic. She explained that her mother had not eaten in the concentration camp either. Her mother refused to budge from her bedside in hospital. It turned out that she was consumed by guilt feelings about her own mother and sister, who had died in the concentration camp. Therapy with the mother created, for the first time, a distance between her and her daughter and resulted in dramatic improvement.

As we might expect, feelings, impulses, even illnesses can be transmitted from one spouse to another.

> Ex. 1(iv). Charny (1992) describes the case of a depressed wife in therapy whose husband repeatedly called the therapist, expressing concern about her worsening condition. The therapist realized that the husband was becoming

depressed, but the latter refused treatment. One day the husband called, fearing his wife might commit suicide. The next morning he killed himself.

Ex. 1(v). Pincus (1976) describes the marriage of Marion and Tony. Marion had an academic career, Tony was a writer who took on a public relations job. Their complementary qualities brought them much joy. He was a bohemian, good with the children, and a good nurse when his wife was ill; she had suffered from asthma since childhood. They would entertain; she did the befriending, he cooked exotic meals. However, there was conflict too; this increased over the years. The more Marion advanced in her work, the more Tony lost interest in his.

When Marion accepted a year's fellowship in a California university, Tony reluctantly agreed. Just before her departure, Tony had alarming asthma attacks, which were new to him. There was now no question of going to California; Marion remained by Tony's side until he had recovered.

Afterwards, exhausted, she had a bad asthma attack, such as she had never had before. She wondered: could she possibly now have his illness just as he seemed to have had hers? She was admitted to the same hospital that had treated Tony. Though considered less ill than he had been, she died within three days.

It seems, then, that impulses, feelings and their somatic expressions can be transferred, apparently mysteriously, from one person to another in a couple or family. They can be 'disowned' by one person and acquired by another. The process by which this happens is known as 'projection', defined as that 'by which specific impulses, wishes, aspects of the self are imagined to be located in some other object external to oneself' (Rycroft 1995, p.139).

In our examples, aspects of one person are not only attributed to another but actually possessed by him or her. Rycroft, indeed, goes on to say that projection may lead to endowing the recipient with aspects of oneself. The concept was first described by Freud and elaborated by Melanie Klein (Rycroft 1995, p.139). We need not go into the complexity of the process here. What is important is to realize that it does occur, and that it therefore makes sense to treat family members in the context of the whole system. As we have seen, treatment of the individual with symptoms often fails; the family as a whole has to be involved.

Systems created for the purpose of therapy

At one time we thought of psychotherapy as something happening between two separate persons: one trained and objective, the other in emotional turmoil or distress. The former can be a detached observer of the latter, as well as treating the person expertly. However, Heisenberg found that the observer affects the object of observation; this most certainly is the case when the object is a human being. Moreover, both patient and therapist have feelings towards one another. We now understand that the patient–therapist dyad is a system given to a complex reciprocal interaction.

There are various therapeutic systems: the dyad of individual therapy, a couple with a pair of co-therapists, or a group. A therapeutic group is unique in that the group members are both subject to treatment, but also, by virtue of the relationship, agents of therapy.

Psychotherapy as relationship

We set up a relationship for the purpose of therapy: we may use a single therapist, or a pair of co-therapists, particularly for couples or families. We may set up a whole group of 'patients' to be therapist; the group as a whole is expected to be therapist to the very members who make it up.

Psychotherapists of various schools of thought differ in their views of the role played by the relationship in therapy. Psychodynamic therapists usually consider it important. Psychoanalysts may believe in the importance of the relationship as such, or consider interpretation the crucial element. The theory that interpretation of transference is the vital element has, in a way, the best of both worlds. This, we know, involves clarifying the ways in which important past relationships are re-enacted in the current therapeutic one.

However, many analysts consider that the nature of the therapeutic relationship itself is what matters. Balint (1969) writes of the importance of the analyst's 'being there', like a mother for the small infant, particularly for patients with a basic fault in the primitive two-person area. Guntrip (1968) holds that the person of the therapist provides a relationship which enables the patient to regress and grow again. He considers that human warmth and concern are essential if the patient is to trust the therapist sufficiently to undergo this painful and frightening process.

Alexander and French (1946) emphasize the corrective emotional experience which depends on the analyst being more tolerant and sympathetic than the parents were in infancy. The anxious patient finds that self-assertion is not punished and begins to 'express himself more freely towards persons in authority in his present life'. Other analysts hold that it would be wrong for the analyst to try to be a better parent than the original parents had been.

Psychotherapy and perception

The way we live is rooted in the way we perceive ourselves and others. One person may see herself as rejected and deprived, another as very much cherished and appreciated. One person may feel driven to achieve more, feeling that he will not be loved unless he does so. It is not a case of 'seeing oneself as one really is', but of having come to see oneself from a particular perspective.

The way we relate to others is based on our perception of them. As Laing, Phillipson and Lee (1965) put it, we are not like billiard balls. We do not react directly to the behaviour of the other, but to our perception of his behaviour. This perception is very subjective: John may be a different person to his various friends, to his wife, to his mother. All these are different from the way he perceives himself.

We have learnt from psychoanalysis that these perceptions of self and others derive from early life experiences. Yet it is not enough to understand how they came about; in fact, an emphasis on causation can encourage a belief in determinism. What is important is to change these perceptions.

Most schools of psychotherapy aim to do so, each in its own particular fashion. Behaviour therapy claims to change nothing but behaviour. In fact, perception of the world is usually changed – by behavioural means. In a cat phobia, perception of cats changes from seeing them as frightening objects to seeing them as friendly, familiar ones. It is not the case that the phobic patient is coerced into merely behaving differently, like a soldier who must face the battle however terrified he feels – at least in most types of behaviour therapy.

Psychoanalysis names 'insight' as one of its aims. This is defined as 'the capacity to understand one's own motives, to be aware of one's own psychodynamics, to appreciate the meaning of symbolic behaviour' (Rycroft 1995, p.81). To be effective, he adds, insight must be emotional and not merely intellectual. 'Although insight refers in the first instance to self-awareness and self-knowledge it is also used to refer to the capacity to understand others.' Insight, then, is a specific case of changing perception. Freud (1924) spoke of the aim of psychoanalysis as making the unconscious conscious. This we might liken to perceiving shapes in what was previously darkness. Insight is one kind of change of perception. One might say it means learning to see aspects of oneself to which one had been blind.

Bateson (1972 [1935], p.300) speaks of 'punctuating reality' in a specific way. To change this is one way of defining perceptual change. He emphasizes that genuine change is a gain in openness: not replacing one view by another, but acquiring the ability to look at reality from different angles.

In one way or another, psychotherapy aims to help patients to see things they had not seen before, or to perceive others (or themselves) in a new way. A mother perceiving her child as difficult and demanding may be asked to explore the child's needs, and see things from a different perspective. She may be asked to look at her own relating with the child, and imagine how it looks from the child's point of view.

A mother had brought a 3-year-old to a child therapy clinic because he was angry and difficult. Seeing a video made of their relating, the mother herself noticed that she was all along stopping the child from doing things the way he wanted. If he wanted to tear up the drawing he had just made, she would stop him. No interpretation was required (G. Elkan, personal communication).

A man who considers himself to have been the deprived child among his siblings is invited to see the opposite side of the coin: he is fortunate not to be overprotected like his brother was. This is an example brought by Schafer (1982), who holds that reconstructing personal narrative is one of the functions of psychoanalysis.

Another possibility would be to see the mother's own difficulties, which led to her being a less than adequate parent. This may lead to feeling some compassion for her and understanding, lessening feelings of self-pity.

There is no one 'right' viewpoint for any person. When a patient says, 'My analyst gave me to understand that...', it is probably a sign of failure. The aim is to enable the patient to see that there are many facets to a situation, and to be able to switch perspectives.

Couples therapy

A husband and wife may have different ways of perceiving things, different concepts of marriage, of how life should be lived, of one another. A failure to realize the possibility of different views can lead to arguments, to accusing the other of deliberately misunderstanding and of malice. Yet conflict can arise and escalate without any bad intention.

> Ex. 1(vi). Sarah and Anthony had come to therapy because of frequent quarrelling. After some improvement, they arrived at one session, announcing: 'We have quarrelled again. We do not understand why.'
>
> Anthony had suggested they go to a film. In the past, Sarah had often disliked the films he chose. He therefore wanted to make sure she approved of his choice. Yet she became angry and eventually refused to come.
>
> Sarah related that her husband repeatedly asked her if she really wanted to go. She understood that he did not really want to take her. She told the children their father was making fun of her.

Marital therapy can help couples to understand that there are different ways of seeing things, and that it is not a matter of 'right' and 'wrong'. It is not so much a matter of agreeing or giving in, but to be released from one's own blinkered viewpoint.

Perception: the case of the Milan School

Consider the work of the Milan School of family therapy (Boscolo *et al.* 1987; Gelcer, McCabe and Smith-Resnick 1990). The therapeutic team formulates a systemic hypothesis that fits the family as a whole. There is no one 'right' view; on the contrary, certainty in the team may lead to their blinding themselves to aspects of the family interaction.

The team endeavours to see the family game from various perspectives. They are helped by their number, as each team member is likely to see things differently. Through questioning the family, it aims to uproot the latter's unexpressed assumptions about themselves, and replace them – not by one 'right' perception, but by the capacity to see things in more than one way. Questions are here preferred to interpretations, since they make the family think for themselves. The Milan School, thus, aims at flexibility of perception.

Psychoanalysts have long thought of the person as being the product of influences in early infancy. This is vertical causation. Yet, as we have more recently come to understand, we are part of the present family, part of the social group, in each of which we fulfil a function. Influences in the family group, the social group, are mutual and reciprocal. This is horizontal causation. Systems theorists and systemic family therapists are familiar with horizontal and circular causation.

The therapeutic group shows such a system at work. Group members take roles (which may change) in the group; they are individuals but also group members, part of the group matrix, fulfilling a function in the group process. In some ways, the group reflects what happens in life outside; this may be a transference phenomenon, or a complete transposition of an outside situation (de Maré, Piper and Thompson 1991). Observing, understanding and working through this is one of the ways in which learning and growth takes place in the group.

CHAPTER 2

Models of Therapeutic Systems

The therapeutic situation may take different forms. It may be a dyad: patient and therapist. It may consist of an existing group of related persons, such as a family or couple, together with a therapist or a pair of co-therapists. It may be a group of persons convened afresh for purposes of therapy, the therapeutic group, with a therapist. Because the individuals in these relationships reciprocally affect one another, these interpersonal situations may be called systems.

Let us represent some of these graphically, using a geometrical analogy.

One-dimensional systems

The oldest and most familiar system is the therapeutic dyad. There is a reciprocal bond between patient and therapist which we can represent as one-dimensional, extension being along one axis (Figure 2.1).

Patient ⟷ Therapist

Figure 2.1 The therapeutic dyad

(In this model, the intrapsychic is represented by a point, having no spatial extension.)

Two-dimensional systems

There are several kinds of two-dimensional systems: the situation of supervision is one example. It is not merely superior experience that characterizes the supervisor's work. What makes it possible for the supervisor to supervise is her perspective on the relationship between student therapist and patient. This creates a second dimension (Figure 2.2).

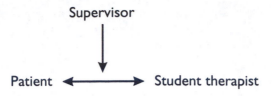

Figure 2.2 Supervision

Often, one notices parallel processes in the two dimensions: what goes on between therapist and supervisor may echo the process between patient and therapist.

Another example of a two-dimensional system is therapy with a couple. First, there is interaction between the spouses – Dimension One. The therapist (or pair of co-therapists) focuses mainly on the relationship between the partners which is reflected in the here-and-now of the treatment situation. We may designate the interaction between therapist(s) and couple as Dimension Two (Figure 2.3).

There is a similar situation in family therapy: Dimension One represents interaction within the family, while Dimension Two represents interaction between family and therapist.

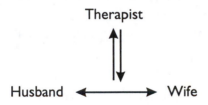

Figure 2.3 Couple therapy

The therapeutic group is another two-dimensional system. Whereas the family is a natural group, the therapeutic group is set up especially for the purpose of therapy. The collection of potential group members has to become a group. The therapist has to make this possible through what might be termed 'negative capability'.

A word about Zero Dimension, the intra-psychic: though not a part of the overt communications in the group, it both feeds into it and is fed by it. An example of the latter is the vicarious treatment process undergone by a silent member.

The basic dimension of interaction is between group members. It includes different kinds of interaction: between two group members, between one member and the group, or involving all group members. We shall call this Dimension One.

There is no lesser unit of interaction within the group. Dyadic interaction between a group member and the therapist prevents the group from doing its own work (or learning to do so). Prolonged dyadic interaction between two group members, if tolerated by the group, serves as a defence against group work (Bion's 'Pairing', 1961).

Dimension Two is between group and therapist (Figure 2.4).

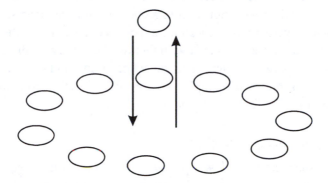

Figure 2.4 The therapeutic group and the therapist

Only part of the events in Dimension Two is communicated. The therapist has a perspective on the group as a whole, and anything that happens within it. Therapists may or may not communicate their observations to the group. Similarly, the group's relating to the therapist (such as transference) may be implicit rather than overt.

We need to stress that Dimension Two is between group and therapist, not between individual members and therapist. The creation of the group is made possible by the therapist's abstinence in this respect. Responding to individual members attempts to create bonds with the therapist makes for a leader-centred group, and for individual therapy within the group.

Three-dimensional systems

Groups made up of groups are three-dimensional. Examples are couples groups and multiple family groups.

Another example is the therapeutic community: it is an added dimension to the small groups, it is always present in the therapeutic space, even when not present in time.

Consider the couples group. Dimension One is the interaction between couples (Zero Dimension being the intra-psychic). Dimension Two is interaction within the group. This may take many forms, for example: between the group and one couple, between couples, between two individuals, between the group and one individual, between men and women (rare). Dimension Three represents all that happens between group and therapist (or pair of co-therapists). More will be said about this in the chapter on couples groups.

In the case of multiple family therapy groups, Dimension One is within families. With families of psychotics, interfamilial communication is often intense, preventing communication with the group as a whole. This is both because of its esoteric nature, and because there seem to be no valencies left. In one such group, I made a rule that families were not to sit together, which minimized some of the whispered and non-verbal communication, and opened the family to the group.

Dimension Two is intra-group: between families, between an individual and a family not his own, between a family and, the whole group, and so on. Dimension Three is between group and therapist(s). More will be said about this in the chapter on multiple family therapy groups.

The nature of the therapeutic dyad

Let us return to the system which is apparently the simplest: the patient–therapist dyad. Freud's original concept was of a neutral, objective analyst observing an individual patient (Figure 2.5).

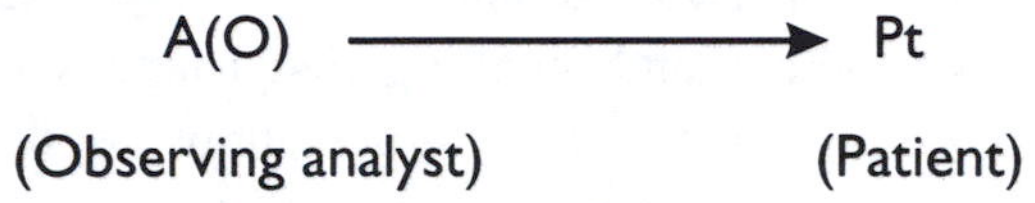

A(O)   ——————————▶   Pt

(Observing analyst)   (Patient)

Figure 2.5 The observing analyst

This was revolutionary: the earlier model had been the medical one, in which a paternalistic therapist actively advised, suggested or hypnotized. With Freud's psychoanalytic model, the therapist renounced some activity to become observer, while the patient was encouraged to be an active participant.

Freud was not content merely to observe the patient's free association; his aim was to treat the patient. This he would do by imparting certain inferences from his observation: interpretations. The observing analyst was also an interpreting analyst (Figure 2.6).

Observing analyst   A(O)
                                Pt
Interpreting analyst   A(I)

Figure 2.6 The dual function of the analyst

Further, Freud found that some of his patients developed strong feelings towards him, and came to the conclusion that they were not really meant for him, but transferred from significant persons in the past. He called the phenomenon transference. The patient was, thus, seeing a fantasy analyst as well as the real analyst (Figure 2.7).

Real analyst   A(R)

Fantasy analyst   A(F)

Pt

Figure 2.7 The dual image of the analyst

Freud advocated that the analyst be as opaque as possible to encourage transference. At first he had believed transference to be an obstacle to treatment; later he found it useful. What happens, in fact, is that the patient is not merely talking about past relationships with significant others, but is demonstrating them, reliving them, in the present (cf. Bateson's model (1972 [1935]), Chapter 6). These past relationships are re-enacted in the transference more vividly and more faithfully than they could have been described, although some decoding may be necessary.

> Ex. 2(i). A young woman in therapy was telling me about recent academic achievements. Suddenly, she burst into tears. 'Whatever I do, it's never good enough for you…it's never enough.'

> I searched my memory for any behaviour on my part that might be interpreted in this way, and could find none. The likelihood was that this was a transference manifestation; she was referring not to me, but to her mother.

Freud noticed that the analyst, too, developed various feelings towards the patient which he called countertransference; he held that they should not be there; the analyst must remain objective. This, for him, was the scientific model.

Science, however, was changing. Einstein formulated his Theory of Relativity, Heisenberg his Principle of Uncertainty.

The latter states: 'In the Gamma Ray microscope, the progress of an electron is watched by scattering Gamma Rays from it with the result that the electron itself is deflected from its original path' (Holton 1973, p.116). To put it another way: 'The scientist…in the act of making measurements, interacts with the observed object and thus causes it to be revealed not as it is, but as a function of measurement' (*Encyclopeadia Britannica*).

Is it justifiable to apply this principle to a human situation? Holton (1973) points out that situations in other sciences are not vague analogies or pale reflections of those in quantum physics, but only one reflection of an all pervasive principle. Ruesch and Bateson (1951) quote Einstein: it is in the social sciences that the coupling between the observed phenomenon and the observer is hardest to minimize.

Applying this understanding to the therapeutic relationship, we recognize that the analyst and patient in therapy form a system in complex mutual interrelations. The analyst is part of the system. The analyst is not merely observing an individual patient but a patient as part of the system, in fact, he or she is observing the system as a whole (Figure 2.8).

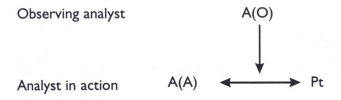

Figure 2.8 The therapeutic system

The 'objective analyst model' fails to take two things into account:

- that the observer is inside the system
- that the act of observation affects the object observed.

When we are inside a stationary train and a train next to us begins to move, we have an illusion that we ourselves are moving. We can, however, determine our stationary position by looking at the landscape on the other side. When we are in a spaceship and another spaceship passes us, we can, with suitable instruments, measure the relative speed at which the other passes us. Nothing, however, can tell us what part of this represents their movement and what part our own movement – or if, in fact, we are moving at all. The psychoanalytic situation is analogous to that of the spaceship.

Later workers, of which Paula Heimann (1950) was a pioneer, understood that 'objectivity' was neither possible nor desirable, and saw in countertransference a means whereby the unconscious of the analyst understands that of the patient. The hubris implied in objective/omniscient observation was abandoned; it was recognized that understanding the patient could be complex and difficult.

This problem is inherent in dyadic therapy – the therapist is observer of the system of which he is a part, and observer of the transference of which he is the object.

The position is slightly different in group-analytic therapy. Here the patient re-enacts situations with significant others in the here-and-now of the group. In so far as this occurs largely in Dimension One, the therapist is in a position to observe it as a relatively detached observer. Nor need the therapist be a lone observer: there may be some group members who notice and comment on this re-enactment. Such interpretations from fellow group members can be very powerful.

This is not to say that observing what happens in a group is not complex. However, experience of convening a group-analytic group bears out what this model suggests: it can be observed with a degree of detachment, and in a perspective not available in dyadic therapy.

CHAPTER 3

The Group as Open System

Anyone who works with the group as a whole – as opposed to the group as background to individual therapy – recognizes that the group is a system, though they may never have heard of system theory. By working with the group as a whole I mean having the ability to perceive group process; I do not mean seeing it as an undifferentiated body, with members being just links in a chain. On the contrary, each member of a therapy group is very much an individual and different from every other. Their individuality is one of the things that makes each group different from every other group.

Bion (1961) concentrated on the group as a whole. He discerned basic processes occurring in the group as a unit. Although he wished to avoid institutionalizing his ideas, his followers have done so, to the point of systematically ignoring the individual member. Ezriel, too, sees the group as one unit: he works exclusively with the transference of the whole group towards the therapist (Ezriel 1973, p.183). As critics have pointed out, these models are really dyadic, since the therapist relates to the group as one homogenous unit.

What I mean by the group being a system is that its members, while remaining individuals, act in ways they could do only in that particular group. They remain themselves but also become group members, and by virtue of this can take on special roles and functions. Their actions and communications are interconnected; for example, a kind of free association occurs between members, so that apparently unconnected communications are found to be connected after all, because they have common unconscious roots. The group can act as a whole; one member may sometimes express feelings on behalf of the whole group.

Foulkes (1948) anticipated system theory in his creation of the therapeutic group and the discovery of its raison d'être. He recognized that the individual person does not function in a vacuum, and could not be treated in isolation. 'As often as not he (the psychiatrist) would, to be sure, find the patient's problems to represent only one aspect of an intricate Group Problem' (Foulkes 1948, pp.21–26). In one case he followed, unconventionally, a patient's suggestion to see the latter's sister-in-law. She proved to be the key to the patient's problem. Since one could not always do fieldwork of this kind, he suggested working with groups in which the patient's problems with others would be reflected.

Foulkes speaks of the 'Group Matrix'. He writes that 'the group-analytic process…rests on an intimate network of communication which gradually grows into an organ-like matrix inside which all processes take place' (Foulkes 1975, p.109). Clearly this is a systems concept.

Systems theory

Let us take a brief look at systems theory. Once, physics had been regarded as the only exact science. As Van Bertalanffy pointed out, there was a need for new concepts for biology, sociology, psychology and economics. Dynamic systems can be found in all of these. 'A system is defined as a complex of components in mutual interaction' (Van Bertalanffy 1966, p.708). Similar principles apply, whatever the nature of the system. Systems theory is an important means for developing exact theory in the non-physical fields of science.

There are closed and open systems. Closed systems are characteristic of inanimate objects, open systems of living creatures. What distinguishes one from the other? In closed systems, entropy (disorder) increases until equilibrium is reached. As a model for entropy, imagine adding a dozen red tennis balls to a dozen white tennis balls in a container. They will become mixed up; it requires an outside agent to sort them out.

In open systems, there is no tendency to entropy. They remain in an orderly, organized state, negative entropy. This is a statistically unlikely condition, made possible by their self-organizing nature.

In open systems, a particular cause does not necessarily have one specific effect. Different initial conditions can lead to the same final state – a phenomenon known as 'equifinality'. For example, in certain animal species it was found that organs grow to their normal size whatever the initial conditions of the embryo.

Equifinality is an important concept in presenting an alternative to linear causality. The idea of a specific cause inevitably leading to a specific outcome implies determinism. Hence it was believed that the only scientific model of humans is the robot model. One form of determinism holds that our actions are determined by unconscious motives, making conscious freedom of the will an illusion. This is the determinism implied in Freudian theory. It leads, however, as Rycroft (1968, pp.27–29) points out, to an internal contradiction: freedom of choice cannot be increased by psychoanalytic treatment if it is non-existent in the first place. Moreover, it implies that consciousness has no function, which is unlikely.

Systems theory gives an alternative model of the person which is no less scientific than the robot model.

Circular causation

The concept of circular causation is familiar, in particular, to family therapists of the Milan systemic school. We owe the concept, originally, to Bateson (1979, pp.115 ff), who gives a model from physics (Figure 3.1).

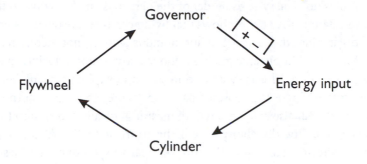

Figure 3.1 Circular causation

To make the system self-correcting, it must be set up in such a way that there is an inverse relation at one of the junctions. For example, the governor might work in such a way that the more the arms diverge, the less the fuel input. If, however, the system is connected in a way 'no engineer would approve of', increasing the fuel supply the more the arms of the governor diverge, it will go into 'runaway', going faster and faster until the machine breaks down.

We can see that some physiological mechanisms resemble this self-correcting model: for example, in the respiratory centre, lack of oxygen increases respiratory activity, excess oxygen decreases it.

Bateson gives models of human relationships analogous to either of these. They may be reciprocal, tending to equilibrium, or 'schismogenic', leading to vicious circles, analogous to 'runaway'. Schismogenic systems might be symmetrical (for example, A and B competing) or complementary(for example, dominant–submissive relating, of individuals or groups). In a couple where one partner was dominant, the other submissive, the dominant would tend to become more dominant, the submissive one more submissive.

The practical importance of circular causation is the realization that no particular person in the relationship is the 'cause' of the problem, and changes made by any of the persons can change the system.

The importance of systems theory for group analysis

Both the systems model of the person and the systems model of the group are important.

The systems model of the person

The stimulus–response model of behaviourism is a robot model, as is the instinct model. Both are based on linear causation, implying determinism, regarding free will as an illusion. The systems model of the person is an alternative to the robot model. Van Bertalanffy (1966) shows that living creatures are open systems. They are self-organizing; they engage in autonomous activity, not merely reacting to stimuli. Man, in addition, engages in symbolic activity, not reducible to instincts; he creates his world. This is evidenced in play and exploration, intellectual and creative activity. There is a sense of past and future, and a true purposiveness; dread of death, but also suicide; a will to meaning, idealistic devotion to a cause, conscience, morality, the ability to tell the truth or to lie. 'All these', as Van Bertalanffy stresses, 'stem from the root of creative symbolic universes and can therefore not be reduced to biology, drives, psychoanalytic instincts, reinforcement or gratification, or other biological functions' (1966, p.714).

Systems and group

All groups are systems, but not all social systems are groups. What characterizes a group? Hopper and Weyman (1973) drew up distinguishing characteristics of groups. Groups frequently meet face to face. They have limited aims and must therefore exist within a larger social system. They are relatively transient and need therefore not be institutionalized. 'Hence, a group differs from an organization because it is not institutionalized' (Hopper and Weyman 1973, p.177).

A group is open to the personality system of its members and also becomes part of their identity, giving a sense of being part of a whole, a sense of 'we'.

Groups tend to be more democratic, less hierarchical, than organizations (Hopper and Weyman 1973).

As far as becoming a part of the members' sense of identity, this is not exclusive to groups. Membership or organizations can contribute to identity, as can religious affiliation or profession. The reverse is not true: the organization does not take on the identity of its members.

I would suggest that institutionalization is the main distinguishing mark between organizations and groups. Therapeutic groups are, in addition, unstructured; there is no hierarchy. All members are of equal status, only the conductor being in a different position. Foulkes (1948) emphasizes the importance of the conductor not being authoritarian, making for a group-centred rather than a leader-centred group.

Even in group situations where there are several staff members, their authority may be deliberately played down. Whiteley (1973) emphasizes this in the case of the large group in the treatment of character disorder. 'A natural learning process evolved and this was enhanced by a deliberate flattening of the institutional hierarchical hospital structure, professional roles were blurred to decrease dependence on medical omnipotence and facilitate the two-way communication of ideas' (p.199).

Thus, therapeutic groups are symmetrical (rather than hierarchical). Whatever their role and social position in life, members have equal status in the group. Each member has the potential of being both the agent and the subject of therapy.

The therapeutic group as open system

Good group therapists are like the man who has been speaking prose all his life and never knew it: they think in system concepts without necessarily calling them by that name. Foulkes appears to have thought of the group as a system without ever using that term.

Some contemporary group analysts have developed the systems aspect of groups. Helen Durkin was a pioneer in this field (J.E. Durkin 1981), as was Yvonne Agazarian (Agazarian and Janoff 1983). In my view, the systems concept is in any case implicit in group-analytic therapy. Let us look at some of its manifestations.

Wholeness

The group comes into being all at once. It cannot be built from a dyad or triad or even two, three or four members. Such aggregates will lack the characteristics of a group and thus tend to disintegrate. Once it has the character of a group, new members may be accepted so that the group will grow larger.

Free-floating discussion and vicarious manifestations

Foulkes pointed to a number of phenomena which in fact characterize it as a system. For example, the basic rule, saying whatever comes to mind, produces free-floating discussion – the equivalent of free association in the individual (Foulkes 1948, p.71). Thus, apparently unconnected communications may have related unconscious roots.

Another phenomenon we can observe is the vicarious expression of feelings. One group member may have expressed anger towards the therapist. Other group members experiencing similar anger will be content to leave it at that; their feelings have been expressed for them.

Foulkes points to the phenomenon of polarization: because one group member takes a certain point of view, another may take the opposite.

Scapegoating can be regarded as an extreme example of such polarization. Swogger (1981, p.70) points out, however, that this and similar phenomena commonly regarded as 'whole group' ones are really a disregard of the group and a reverting to dyadic relationship ('If it weren't for him...'). We might regard scapegoating as an example of black/white thinking. This fits in with de Maré's concept of the group, particularly the larger one, as able to transcend the digital, binary, Aristotelian logic of black/white, encompassing an analogic logic involving a rainbow of colours and a range of possibilities (De Maré *et al.* 1991). Heaping all the blame on to one group member is a regression to black/white thinking.

The therapeutic group as an unstructured system

We have emphasized that the therapeutic group at its best is open to a wide range of possibilities. This openness tends to create anxiety. Hopper and Weyman (1973) distinguish between simple and complex groups. In complex groups, there is differentiation, division of labour, and usually a hierarchy. Roles tend to be specific. In contrast, simple groups show little differentiation; roles tend to be diffuse. As an example of specific roles the authors give those of bank manager and client; diffuse roles are those of parents and children; siblings; therapist and patient; good teacher and student.

It is interesting to consider this in the light of Buber's (1937) modes of relating. Diffuse roles seem to correspond to the 'I–Thou' mode, while specific roles correspond to the 'I–It' mode.

How does the therapeutic group fit into this scheme? I suggest that it is characterized by being undifferentiated, with roles being diffuse. This diffuseness makes for openness and change in the group, though it also arouses anxiety. Both group and individual member may fear this openness to infinite possibilities, especially at the beginning of a new group. Bion (1961) has demonstrated some typical defences against group anxiety, which might be seen in this light: dependency, fight and flight, pairing. There is, however, another kind of defence against the anxiety of undifferentiation: the adoption of specific roles, to the point of their becoming stereotypes.

In the ordinary course of events, the individual who becomes a group member may take on all sorts of roles that might not have otherwise presented themselves: patient, listener, leader, therapist, champion of the disadvantaged, child, mother, father and more. She can become a sympathetic listener, more so than she would have been in a social situation. She could, on the other hand, become a needy child, grateful for the help of others. She can, if she feels safe enough, become angry at something that is happening in the group. She can allow herself to be fatherly or motherly towards a group member not necessarily younger than her.

When these roles are temporary and fluid, they serve a constructive purpose. They can, however, become frozen.

> Ex. 3(i). In a slow-open group of psychotic outpatients, Daniel was a newcomer. He had never been treated in hospital, and was rather less sick than most of the other members. He was religious, and tended to quote the Bible and other sources when a question was asked. Probably because of these characteristics, the group soon came to regard him as their adviser and their guru. Daniel happily fell into the role. He had the answers; he would soothe and advise.
>
> The group and he both enjoyed the situation and appeared to benefit. There was, however, a price: Daniel did not bring his own problems to the group – he was the guru, after all. It took some time before Daniel felt safe enough to abandon the exclusivity of his role and begin to bring his own problems.

It is clear in this example that both Daniel and the group contributed to this 'freezing' of his role. In the following example, the group was more sophisticated, but may still have played a part in role stereotyping.

> Ex. 3(ii). In a group of five couples, Tessa always brought her husband as 'the patient' in the family. In relating to others in the group, she specialized in psychological explanations. She resisted all invitations by the group or the therapists to talk about herself. When she did, it would be something like: 'I have decided not to put up with my husband's behaviour...'. Only on one occasion did she talk about her own childhood, and how sad it had been to see her mother's depression.
>
> In this group, Tessa used the role of 'psychologist', with a variant of 'long-suffering wife', in the service of resistance against becoming involved in the group.

Stereotyped roles serve to diminish anxiety, both for the group and for the patient who takes on – or allows himself to be pushed into – a role. Though it may be in varying degrees, both the role-taking member and the group as a whole play a part in the process. However, stereotyped roles block the development and expression of individuality and negate authenticity. They inhibit the process of change and creativity in the group.

The nature of causality in the work of the group

Foulkes wrote of group-analytic therapy (1975, p.124): 'There is no active search for the past, but it comes dynamically into the situation.' Since we know that group members tend to behave towards the group as they did towards significant others in the past, work is useful on the here-and-now. This puts the accent on the possibility of change, rather than the sense of determinism that sometimes arises from stressing the exploration of causes in the past. ('If I am like this because of what happened to me as a child, how can I change?')

System theorists working with groups stress the importance of 'equifinality', the notion that different causes may lead to the same effect. Admittedly, this still says nothing about the possibility of one cause having different effects. It does, however, question the rigid 'one cause – one effect' sequence derived from the concept of causality in the inanimate world.

Circular causality

The recognition of circular causality in the therapeutic group is important. When a group member acts in a particular way in a group, and continues to do so, the group also has a part in this: it is allowing or even encouraging this. The phenomenon that Bion (1961) described as 'pairing' is an example; though only two members engage in it – one might say indulge in it – the group allows it to continue when one would expect it to object. (Bion concentrates entirely on the role of the group in this.)

Acknowledging circular causation is important: interpretation can be directed both at the specific member and at the whole group. If a group member monopolizes the group, the therapist might usefully ask the group why it is allowing this. If a member in apparent distress is holding the whole group to ransom, without really making use of it, interventions can be directed to both group and group member.

> Ex. 3(iii). As soon as she joined the group, Anna found it hard to speak. In the first four sessions she said nothing at all; then she began to communicate her problems. She spoke about her loneliness, her fear of making a relationship with men. She spoke of her childhood and her mother's cruelty. Anna was single; she had begun to train as a nurse but had given up after a year. She now worked in an office.
>
> It happened again that Anna came to the group obviously wanting to speak, but apparently unable to do so. The rest of the group, after trying to encourage her, fell silent, apparently feeling that their own problems were minor in the light of her overwhelming ones. Anna was certainly distressed, but also sensed and possibly enjoyed her power to silence the group at such times. Interpretation had to be directed both at her and at the group as a whole; both had a part in the situation.

A system theory of energy transformation

Walter Gruen's theory of change in the group is simple and acceptable (described in Durkin 1981). We can define entropy as a form of energy unavailable for work

– for example, locked up in intrapsychic conflict. Living systems can reorganize themselves to new levels with more available energy.

One way of doing this is through psychotherapy, in which the therapist provides a 'sanctuary-like' situation in which the faulty organization can be examined, and the nurturant energy of the therapist made available.

In the group situation, the therapist's task is to ensure that interaction does not simply use up all available energy. (This, in Foulkes' terminology, is the therapist's function as 'dynamic administrator', who provides suitable conditions for the group to work. The therapist usefully intervenes when interaction is unproductive or destructive.) Gruen gives an example of available energy being used up: one patient being depressed, a second one yelling at him, while a third becomes anxious about the situation.

Having no agenda, Gruen continues, means that the therapist's energy is indeed available. We might think of it as the therapist having no needs of his own, being open to whatever needs arise in the course of the group process.

These are just some of the manifestations of the systems character of the group. It may be a case of translating well-known phenomena into the language of systems theory. I hope that I have shown that Foulkes regarded the therapeutic group as a system, and worked with it on that basis. This is in contrast to schools of thought who hold the group to be background to individual therapy.

CHAPTER 4

Aspects of the Group Relationship

What makes the group effective as a therapeutic agent? Let us consider two important aspects: the first is the nature of the group relationship. The second is the difference it makes to members' perceptions of self and others.

The nature of the group relationship

Every therapeutic system involves a relationship of which clients can avail themselves in various ways. The group, by its nature, has potentially more to offer than the therapeutic dyad.

This is not immediately obvious. Uninitiated patients (and therapists) may believe that a group is 'second best'. They may argue that the group member receives only a small share of the therapist's attention. But this is to miss the point. The group is therapeutic in many ways that dyadic therapy can never offer (as I hope to show in subsequent chapters). The group gives a sense of belonging, it is perceived as a mother figure, caring and accepting, in some ways giving a feeling of greater security than any individual therapist can give. Patients who have defected from individual therapy, or been irregular attenders, may come regularly to a group, once it has become cohesive. On a wet and stormy day, most of the members of my group of schizophrenic outpatients showed up.

The group is a microcosm, as Yalom (1981) put it; the various relationships of the individual member are reflected in it. As a group member said: 'We behave in the group as we behave in life.' It can function as a mirror, showing members how others respond to their mode of relating. It is a field for trying out new ways of relating to others. The timid person, the one whose voice is never heard, can begin to learn to make themselves heard in the group.

Hegel (1910) said that self-consciousness requires 'an object against which to differentiate itself' (Singer 1983, p.57). A group provides objects against which to differentiate oneself. Being in a group encourages self-definition and thus furthers individuation. (This is particularly true of median sized groups of around twelve to twenty members.)

Unlike natural groups in life, the therapeutic group begins only when convened and ceases to exist when disbanded. However, the group, once it becomes cohesive, is internalized. This inner group continues to be there between meetings, during vacations, and may go on for some time after the group terminates. Unlike the family, the group becomes an entity all at once, by meeting as a whole (in accordance with the principles of systems theory). One cannot gradually build a group from two members, in the way that a family begins with a couple. However, new members can join the once established group without essentially changing its character.

It takes time for a group to become cohesive. Cohesiveness arises from the feeling of each member that he or she belongs to the group and that it is important to him or her. It implies reciprocity, giving and receiving: the member feels responsibility for the group on the one hand, and receives benefits from it on the other. (Members who expect the group to be there for them whenever they choose to come have not grasped this vital principle.) In a successful group, members feel responsible for the group along with the therapist. They might, for example, call members who have been absent to find out whether there is anything wrong. In one couples group, members who could not attend would call others to discover whether there would be enough to make a group, or whether to suggest to the therapist to cancel the session.

The cohesive group is internalized by the group member; he takes it home within himself; it is present for him at difficult times. This inner group does not depend on the presence of any particular member; it does not even require the presence of the therapist.

Because of their sense of belonging together, some groups meet, leaderless, in between times or during holidays. The group I observed at the Tavistock Clinic in the 1960s would meet in the pub after each session. Mullan and Rosenbaum (1973) held that one might as well encourage the alternative meeting, without the convener. In the case of one couples group I was running with a co-therapist, we decided not to continue with just one therapist during a year I would be absent on study leave. On return, we discovered that the group had, on their own initiative, met every week in the house of each of them in turn.

The therapy group is a system, a group of persons in a dynamic relationship. We learn from systems theory that open systems – as living systems are – are not static, but in dynamic equilibrium.

Stability and change

The aim of the therapeutic group is to be an agent of change. In order to be so, it has to have some stability. The therapeutic group is rather more stable than the individuals composing it. There can, however, be too much stability; some long-standing closed groups come to be 'stuck', having ceased to encourage change and make it possible. In some cases at least, it seems that they have unwittingly learnt to collude to avoid painful subjects; not to tread on one another's toes.

The situation is in a sense analogous to that of the family: cohesiveness is valued and gives a sense of security. When cohesiveness becomes enmeshment, and stability becomes inflexibility, a price is paid: it becomes more difficult for children to find their own identity and autonomy.

Not every non-natural group is an agent of change. The ideological group is often designed to prevent change, or to channel it in a predetermined direction. In contrast, the therapeutic group cannot have a predetermined aim, as its function is to enable each individual member to grow and develop in his own way. Thus, as de Maré (1984) phrased it, the group personifies creativity, a journey into the unknown.

The group develops its therapeutic capacity

Under favourable conditions, the group itself undergoes slow processes of growth and change. It develops a capacity for imaginative understanding of others, as well as genuine criticism and often surprising insight. It conduces to the development, to an increasing degree, of a sense of belonging, of mutual trust, of tolerance and often a good deal of caring for one another. It develops the capacity for group dialogue, which implies a sense of mutuality, as well as the ability to listen and to express oneself.

Each group develops a group culture which has its own 'personality', though all group cultures possibly have features in common. The group culture has phases like the culture of a nation: a ten-year-old slow-open group has a culture that is more mature than a two-year-old one. The population will gradually have changed, but the culture is handed on.

The group is able to do many things better than the therapist can. Unlike the therapist, it has not been taught that one ought not to be too supportive. It can be reassuring today and critical tomorrow, or both at the same time, different members taking different positions. Its criticism is often more acceptable than that of the therapist, coming from 'one of us'. It can take a member by the hand and help her, in a way that a therapist could never allow herself to do.

Ex. 4(i). Yoram, the 35-year-old father of two children, had been a self-employed craftsman before he became depressed. He worked less and less, with orders falling off until he had to close shop. A burglary in the workshop added to his losses. Yoram refused to claim National Insurance, arguing that he did not want to be a burden on anyone. This was indeed a dominant theme with him: he was concerned that he was now useless and merely a burden on his family. He was reluctant to burden the group with his misery. The group gently and patiently encouraged him to talk about himself. When they realized that he was unable or unwilling to make a move to get help, one member arranged to go along with him to the necessary office, and this worked. Another, a civil servant, made inquiries regarding nursery care for his children; this too was effective in enabling Yoram to accept help from outside sources.

Before joining the group, Yoram had been in individual therapy. He had absented himself frequently, whereas he came to the group regularly. At first, he seemed to feel guilty for occupying space, as it were. Gradually, with the help of the group, he overcame this feeling.

Enough has been said to indicate that the therapeutic group can provide a rich and secure therapeutic relationship. It can give the group member a sense of belonging, make him feel valued, give support and hope. Its stability may make it safe for the individual member to change and grow, without in any way pushing him.

The quality of the group relationship

In individual therapy, many workers believe that it is the nature of the therapeutic relationship that is crucial for change. Guntrip (1968) holds that a secure individual therapeutic relationship enables the patient to regress to an early infantile stage and grow anew. I suggest that this is no less true of the group, which has the power to hold and contain the individual. Yalom (1981) holds that group cohesiveness is not in itself curative, but is a precondition for change; he finds other factors that make for change. Be that as it may, the group relationship is of major importance to the individual member. It becomes a presence which is mostly perceived as benevolent, understanding, tolerant and caring – though it can be perceived as critical and even threatening by some. Group members speak of the group as 'being with them' when they are physically away from it, when alone and perhaps in a difficult situation. The group is thus internalized as a good object. Ada Abraham (personal communication) speaks of the 'good group' as a refuge and a means of coping with the relatively anonymous and indifferent larger group outside.

The therapy group has often been compared to a mother who provides for one's needs. How is it possible for the group to cater for all the different individuals that make up its membership? While the individual therapist needs the sensitivity to provide the needed relationship for the person in therapy, the group has another quality: because of its heterogeneity, the individual member can usually find in it what he or she requires. It is flexible and many-sided.

To sum up, the group by just 'being there' can be very important to the individual member. It may take a long time before members feel sufficiently secure to speak of the really important things, to embark on the painful exploration of their inner world. Nonetheless, it is their trust in the group which makes it possible to do so.

Transference and transposition

There are more specific ways in which the group relationship becomes part of the therapeutic process. It has been found that members re-enact, toward the group, their mode of relating to important others in life. (This may refer to present or past relating, though present relationships are often a repetition of those with significant others in infancy.) This phenomenon has been called 'transference to the group', as it is analogous to transference in the therapeutic dyad. De Maré, Piper and Thompson (1991) prefer to call it 'transposition', since, after all, a whole situation of 'there-and-then' is transposed to the 'here-and-now'. This term has the advantage of distinguishing the phenomenon from transference to the group conductor.

Yalom (1981) speaks of the group as a social microcosm, referring, as I understand it, to the same phenomenon, with the stress on present relationships. He emphasizes that the group member's mode of relating to the outer world is reflected in his way of relating to the group. The individual member can thus observe and receive feedback from the group as to how he relates to others and what effect this has on them. The here-and-now aspect is indeed fruitful in the group, rather than tracing back transference to its historic roots in each individual.

Whatever terminology we favour, it is useful to think of transference as manifesting itself in space, the space of the group, rather than in time.

As an object of transference or transposition, the group has several advantages over the dyadic relationship.

First, in the dyadic situation, the analyst is inside the situation he observes: he is both transference object and observer of the transference. Moreover, he has to disentangle transference phenomena from manifestations of the real relationship. In the group, the strands are less tangled. In the case of transference to the therapist, the group is there to observe it and provide perspective. Transposition to the group is usually evident both to the group and to the therapist. When it is directed towards one member, it is easily observable by the rest of the group.

Second, in dyadic therapy, the patient is by definition unaware of his transference to the analyst, at least initially. Transference is the unconsciously determined perception of the analyst as someone he is not. One task of transference interpretation is to help him realize this. This realization may be quite difficult to achieve.

The problem is compounded when transference is negative, when the patient may not accept interpretations. The patient may feel a need to devalue the analyst's work and reject interpretations. Since transposition to the group is so easily observable, the individual member concerned may also see it more easily. 'Transference interpretations' made by the group may be more acceptable than similar ones made by the therapist.

Third, in dyadic therapy, the communication and understanding of transference interpretations is an intellectual process. In the group, transposition occurs *in vivo*, is observable by all, and requires no historical speculations to validate it.

As the group is a multi-person situation, relationships of dyad, triad or a larger group of persons can be transposed into it. In dyadic therapy, only dyadic relationships can be reflected through transference. The third person is perceived as one too many, creating a conflict situation, the Oedipal triangle. Larger relationships cannot be observed at all, only talked about. In life, however, there are satisfying as well as vicious triangles. The mother–father–child triangle is basically a good one; Oedipal rivalry exists but does not negate its benign potential. There are others: two interrelating and one watching, a three-sibling group or a three-friend group. Bowen (1964) found that triangles are formed to reduce tension in the case of difficult two-person relationships.

Configurations greater than three play a significant part in our lives. Witness the group of four or five close friends, often becoming important in adolescence, as one kind of small group. Then there is the larger peer group which is no less significant, be it youth movement, student group, political group, or simply 'the gang', for better or for worse. The adolescent uses the peer group in the process of separating from her family and finding her identity. In later life, it may be the group of colleagues at work which is important. In some cases, the person has to face a group in an asymmetrical situation, as teacher of a class of children or students, or as director of a group of staff.

The exact number, as Simmel (1950) points out, matters less and less as the group increases in size. The object relations technique (ORT) projective test classifies relationships into one-, two- or three-person or group, pictorially represented by five to eight people. The significance of larger groups has only been recognized relatively recently (Kreeger 1973).

The large group tends to have a faceless, anonymous quality which poses a threat to identity (Turquet 1973). It can arouse an experience akin to psychosis. It lends itself to various possibilities. It can explore aspects of the psychology of a larger group in life, such as a community or organization. It thrives on metaphor, imagery and humour. It can generate group dreams over a number of sessions, or illuminate ideas and views by dint of its multiple perspectives. On the other hand, when there are grounds for it, the group might argue over here-and-now reality issues. It is most often used as a training ground for learning about large group dynamics, but can become the mainstay of work in a therapeutic community (Whiteley 1973).

Work with larger groups brought out a distinction between large and median groups. De Maré's median group is larger than a small group, but small enough for every person in it to get to know the others, and for every person to participate in the dialogue. It is run as a slow-open group-analytic group. It can reflect the individual's relationship to society, as well as more intimate ones. It initially arouses feelings of anxiety and even hate which become transformed into an anonymous kind of friendship de Maré calls 'koinonia', by its Greek term (De Maré *et al.* 1991). This kind of group is particularly qualified to allow the individual member to be 'different'.

What interests us is the reflection of real-life groups in therapeutic groups. Any group smaller than itself or similar in size can be transposed into the therapeutic/training group. For the small group, this means the dyad, triad or small natural group, including the family. For the larger group, all these as well as larger group relationships (such as workplace groups, organizations, political groups).

The group also has an advantage in its capacity to analyse and interpret transposition in the fullest way: members have different personalities and different roles in life. They therefore have different viewpoints and can see aspects of the group members' relating from various angles.

To sum up, the therapeutic group is particularly helpful to the understanding of transference or transposition to the group, for various reasons: because the process is easily observable, because object and observer of transference are not necessarily identical (as in individual therapy), and because it is large enough to reflect any configuration smaller than or equal to itself.

CHAPTER 5

The Individual and the Group

Separateness and Belonging

There is a bipolar quality to many of our deepest needs, and they may appear paradoxical. Just as we feel a need for tension and relaxation, the stimulus of the new and the safety of the old, our interpersonal needs are bipolar. We have a need to belong, to be included and to be accepted by our group; at the same time we feel that it is vital to remain distinct, different and an individual. The distance from either pole at which we feel at ease varies with personality and culture. The accent of individuality in society, on self-determination, is a modern and relatively recent development. In earlier times, the person was regarded more as a member of society than as an individual, and in some cultures this still tends to be the case. Durkheim (1952) describes 'altruistic' suicide in such cultures, which is really a resignation from individual life for the sake of the social group. An example is the obligatory suicide of the aged in some societies.

There are individual differences: belonging is more important to some persons, separateness and aloneness to others.

We tend to feel a need to 'be one of' our current group, not to be excluded by them. Rejection, scorn and ridicule are painful, appreciation and support comforting. The sense of being part of a larger whole becomes important. This begins with the peer group of children in kindergarten, possibly earlier. (The sibling group is important in a different way, with a special closeness as well as rivalry.) Next comes the school class, the adolescent peer group, which may be a specially chosen and exclusive small group of friends, or a larger group. One may join a political party, in which case the sense of belonging to the group can be a driving force to action. We are willing to give of our time and energy voluntarily, for the sake of contributing to a larger whole, a group in whose cause we believe. There is the student group; the peer group at the place of work. Most people feel a need to 'belong' to several groups at any period in their lives: it might be a social group, and the group of colleagues at work (unless one works alone). One does not want to be 'out of it', to be regarded as 'different', wants to be part of 'us'. One may, in addition, choose to belong to a leisure group in which the social element is more or less prominent. I was struck by the social structure of my folk dance group in which there was no competition and all were of equal status – very refreshing after competitiveness at work. One day I proposed the composition of a new dance melody for the teacher to choreograph. I was given to understand that this was not wanted. The implicit reason, I believe, was that it would have made me 'special'.

Both the need and the opportunity for individuation and differentiation are in a sense a function of being part of a group, as we shall see. Robinson Crusoe had neither a need nor an opportunity to be different.

Individuality and the group

One may imagine that the price of belonging to a group is conformity. Is this indeed the case? With what kinds of groups? Does it apply to the therapeutic group? When Freud (1921) writes of group psychology he refers to the institutions of the Church and the army, which are highly organized (cf. groups and organizations, Chapter 3.) It is noteworthy that Freud used the word *Massenpsychologie*, crowd psychology, which was mistranslated 'group psychology'.

We merge in a crowd, losing individuality; there is no pressure to conform, but the crowd is amorphous. On the other hand, groups which are highly organized, and institutionalized, tend to demand a degree of conformity. They do so particularly when they aim to preserve an ideology or create a group identity, they require conformity. This may conflict with development of individuality by their members. Deviance is not tolerated.

Consider the Church, a highly institutionalized group. In Morris West's *The Shoes of the Fisherman*, a Vatican brother writes a philosophical work after prolonged study and reflection. The Church regards the ideas presented in it as heretical. The brother is faced with the choice of leaving the group, or denying his work of many years.

Professional organizations may have less explicit rules, yet some lay great stress on conformity. For example, psychoanalytic training institutes may require adherence not only to specific rules, but also to ways of thinking. Because it is important for members to belong, both technically and emotionally, they tend to conform.

Despite the tensions it brings about, individual difference, non-conformity and creativity benefit the group that can accept it, and keeps it from stagnation. Some analysts in the British Psychoanalytic Society, who were unable to adopt the dogmatism of the Freudian and Kleinian schools, formally broke away and called themselves 'Middle Group', later 'The Independent Stream'. Yet many professed Freudian analysts study Winnicott or Rycroft (both Independents) and consider that the discipline has been enriched by their 'deviant' contributions.

In a discussion programme on Israel television (in the 1980s), the issue was the attitude of the Kibbutz to the 'odd man out', the member who rejects the conventions of the group. Some spoke of the problems so created, others of the need for tolerance. Two 'odd men (or women) out' saw themselves as outsiders. One Kibbutz member (representing the 'rank and file') made the point that the existence of non-conformists was important for the vitality of the Kibbutz. The structure of the Kibbutz is unusual in that positions of responsibility are rotating, thus preventing stratification. The individual Kibbutz is therefore not an organization (though it may belong to an organization). Important decisions are taken by the whole group in weekly meetings. Features like communal dormitories for children have been modified, while others were regarded as essential to the identity of the Kibbutz. (At the time of writing some Kibbutzim are in the process of abandoning this identity, while others decided to cling to basic principles.)

What kind of a group is the group-analytic group? It is neither a crowd nor an organization, but a group characterized by face-to-face communication. It has no extraneous function or purpose: it exists solely for the sake of its members. Hence it does not demand conformity. As Foulkes (1948) put it,

> the sound part of individuality, of character, is firmly rooted in the Group and wholly approved by it. The Group, therefore, respects and supports the emergence and free development of individuality, and Group treatment has nothing to do with making people uniformly march in step. Quite the contrary, good Group treatment – by developing a good Group – makes both processes go hand in hand: the reinforcement of the communal ground and the freer development of individual differences. Like a tree – the firmer it takes root the freer it can display its individual characteristic beauty above ground. (Foulkes 1948, p.30)

The group helps to define identity

Being in a therapy group, indeed, makes definition of identity possible. As opposed to a vague comparison with dimly perceived others that may make us feel we ought to be all alike, the direct view afforded by the group gives permission to be different, to be ourselves.

More than that, the sense of identity depends, first, on the presence of another from which to differentiate oneself, and second, on recognition by others. As Hegel held, self-consciousness cannot exist in isolation, but 'requires an object from which to differentiate itself. I can only become aware of myself if I am also aware of something that is not myself' (Singer 1983, p.57). R.D. Laing (1961) pointed out that the sense of identity depends on complementarity. 'The good breast is a breast that can receive as well as give… Emptiness and futility can arise when a person…is accorded no recognition by the other, and if he feels he is not able to make any difference to anyone' (Laing 1961, p.67). Denial of recognition of a person by her significant others can bring about the total destruction of her sense of identity.

The needs described can be filled by the therapeutic group: to differentiate oneself from others, to be perceived and recognized by others. The group situation makes it possible to make a difference to others, even for persons who are themselves needy and thirsty for help.

Difficulties of individuals in 'belonging'

Some persons have difficulty in making a relationship, experiencing anxiety that in doing so they might lose themselves. Laing (1960) points to the dilemma of the schizoid: relationship brings the threat of 'impingement', 'implosion' or 'engulfment', while remaining isolated holds another threat, of shut-upness, of living only mentally with no enrichment from outside. Such people have also been described as having 'fragile ego boundaries'. Guntrip (1968, p.36) describes the dilemma of the schizoid individual who 'can neither be in a relationship with another person nor out of it'.

It may be difficult to help such people, as they cannot commit themselves to a therapeutic relationship. In some cases, it is easier for them to be part of a group than a dyad; they can control the emotional distance at which they find themselves at any point. Simmel (1950) points out that some types of persons prefer groups to dyads, and vice versa. In my experience, schizoids often do well in median groups, which makes it possible for them to be 'in' or 'out', involved or uninvolved. This is not invariable; some feel marked anxiety at being in a group at all.

The group as a basis for individuation

It is often believed that individuation is better nurtured in individual therapy rather than in the group. The group is believed to demand conformity to a norm, while individual therapy is custom-made for the individual, as it were. The model for dyadic therapy one has in mind may be individual teaching. Most people learn to play an instrument in individual lessons, the teacher adapts the teaching to each pupil's specific problems and abilities, to his own pace. Learning in a class seems to be a disadvantage. Consider, on the other hand, the learning of philosophy. The questions and views of other members of my class clearly add a great deal to my understanding. Even in music a class may have advantages, as personal experience testifies. I studied composition in a class with the British composer Alan Bush. One of his assignments was to write a string quartet according to the form of the opening of Shostakovich's Quartet no. 8. By setting limitations, he gave us a lot of freedom in the space defined. It was also illuminating to hear how other class members dealt with the task.

In dyadic therapy, two things are lacking. In the first place, the patient has no idea how others cope with a particular situation. He has no real idea whether he is unique in his eccentricity, in the grossness of his problem, as it seems to him. He may feel he is deviating from some imaginary norm, a norm he has read about or heard about or imbibed with his mother's milk. In the group, however, it is easy to see that people have very different styles of dealing with particular issues. It becomes permissible to be different, to be one's own person.

The second problem is that every therapist, by virtue of being human, has personal assumptions about social norms, some of which may be unconscious. They exist however hard we may try to be neutral and objective. Let me illustrate this with an anecdote from the life of the neurologist and anthropologist W.H. Rivers (Barker 1991). He asked a group of islanders what they would do if they found or earned a guinea – would they share it? At some point they turned the tables on him; they asked him the same question. When he said he was unmarried and saw no need to share it at all, they began to laugh; this seemed very strange to them. 'He suddenly realized that their reactions to his society were neither more or less valid than his to theirs and saw not only that we weren't the measure of all things, but that there was no measure' (Barker 1991).

Any group may, of course, have its own bias, its own prejudices. In one experiential group for professionals the motto was: 'Speak for yourself, do not discuss the group process.' In another group of the same kind, this did not feature at all. Every group has its own culture, and has developed tacit precepts of what should and should not be done in the course of the group. But the group culture is less concerned with styles of coping in life, outside the group. Being made up of different individuals, it is highly likely that the group will express a range of viewpoints on any issue.

The group thrives on individual difference

Individual difference between members is the driving force of the group process. A is strong on what is B's weakness, whereas C is in a position to help A in another area. C and D have one quality in common and differ in another. Groups which are homogenous in psychopathology or personality type are likely to lose out on this dynamic quality.

To sum up, the therapeutic group encourages the development of individuality on several grounds:

- Individuality is the condition for the continued existence of the group.

- Personality finds expression only in relation to others, ideally in a group.
- The group gives feedback on difference
- As it consists of numerous members, it is likely to be more pluralistic than any single therapist can be.

The analogy with individual development

Piaget (1932) shows that personality is developed through association with the peer group rather than through the parent–child relationship. In the stage when only the parents are important to the child, respect is unilateral, rules of conduct are accepted because of parental authority. At that stage 'the child has no idea of his own ego', 'he does not distinguish the part played by his subjectivity from that played by environmental pressure' (Piaget 1932, p.90).

As children grow, around the age of 7 or 8, they learn to relate to their peers. Obeying authority figures becomes less important than cooperation with equals.

> Henceforth he will not only discover the boundaries that separate his self from the other person, but will learn to understand the other person and be understood by him. So that cooperation is really a factor in the creation of personality, if by personality we mean, not the unconscious self of childish egocentrism, nor the anarchical self of egoism in general, but the self that takes up its stand on the norms of reciprocity and objective discussion, and know-how to submit in order to make itself respected. (Piaget 1932, p.90)

We may regard dyadic therapy as analogous to the parent–child relationship, group therapy to the peer group relationship.

Belonging

Belonging to a group is a reciprocal relationship. The individual makes a move to enter the group (which involves more than just sitting there). The group accepts him; he accepts responsibility for membership (which begins with regular attendance). The group comes to accept responsibility for him.

The group at first accepts the individual on faith: He may be ugly and consider himself unloved and unlovable. It does not matter to the group that he is unsuccessful or deviant. I have seen homosexuals accepted with ease, with gestures of welcome extended by those whose religious principles forbade homosexuality. On the other hand, a group might be inclined to reject a member who believes he is perfect and has nothing to learn.

Breaking the rule is another reason for rejection. These are implicit, and include fairness, sincerity, mutual consideration and confidentiality.

Ex. 5(i). Max joined a group of outpatients, most of whom had been psychotic. He talked a lot, often overriding others who had not finished speaking. He once remarked that he was superior to the others: he was not crazy, he was merely on probation. He seemed quite impervious to the feelings of others. He visited the house of a woman group member uninvited and would not desist. After a month, the group told him that they could not tolerate this kind of behaviour.

Ex. 5(ii). In the same group, at a different point in time, Ninette had been a member for almost a year. She visited a social club to which other group members also belonged. On one occasion, it turned out that she had been disclosing information about Tony, another group member, in the club: she had told someone that his son was a drug addict and serving a prison sentence. The group was furious. Some talked about leaving the group, as it was no longer safe to be in it. The members mentioned that Ninette had let her tongue run away with her on a previous occasion and had been warned.

The rule of confidentiality had never been spelt out, but it was quite clear to the group that it was a rule. I decided that the only fair decision, and the only way to restore the group's feeling of safety, was to ask Ninette to leave the group.

Group members being human, they are not invariably as accepting as they ought to be. Talking about M., a new member absent on that day, they said: 'She is not like us. She does not belong here.' M. in fact suffered from minimal brain damage and was perseverative and clinging in her manner. She did need the group, or a group, but it seemed that she might be better accepted in a different one.

The very fact that acceptance by a group is not automatic, that it has to be earned, makes it more valued. A therapist has to be accepting, it is part of her professional code. The group has no such obligation. (Note that Max in Ex. 5(i) was rejected on the grounds of his behaviour towards the group.) Tony (Ex. 5(ii)) was a man diagnosed as character disorder. As he made it his business to be attentive and considerate to others, he earned his place in the group and there was no question of rejecting him. There were moments when he was demanding and irritating, or lost his temper. As he had enough 'credit' in the group, these crises were worked through.

In the first stage, the group accepts the new member 'on faith'. In the second stage, it extends empathy, understanding, consideration and caring to the individual member when the need arises.

Ex. 5(iii). Kenneth was a member of a median sized group (which contained students of group analysis as well as patients). He told the group that a woman had talked to him at a bus stop. As he considered that he was unlovable, he wondered why anyone would want to talk to him at all; he hated the face he saw in the mirror. Anne said she thought it was a nice face; she would certainly want to talk to him. Kenneth had not spoken in the group for many weeks; he did sub-

sequently take part in the dialogue. No doubt it was the warmth and understanding of the group that made it possible.

The reciprocal aspect of acceptance is the individual member's sense of
belonging. This is not merely an awareness of being accepted and belonging: it
involves responsibility. There are group members who claim the right to come
once in two weeks to a weekly group, failing to realize that the existence of the
group depends on their presence, on the presence of all members.

The second stage, from the member's point of view, is trust in the group. This
takes time to develop. It depends both on the member's ability to trust, and the
trustworthiness of the group. Unless members trust the group, they cannot expose
their weakness or talk of their more painful feelings.

The strength of feeling is not necessarily equal on either side. A member may
be the focus of much care and concern and yet feel little sense of responsibility
towards the group. Helen, a schizophrenic woman, would come to the group once
in two weeks or fewer times. When she did come, she behaved as if it were there
mainly for her (or rather as if the therapist were there just for her; I would redirect
her questions to the group). She asked for advice and assurance. When asked to
relate to others, she would do so, though she naturally had missed the thread of
what was happening to them. It did not occur to her that she might be missed by
the group when absent. In part, this was due to her abysmally low self-esteem. She
did not believe that she could make a difference to anyone. Schizophrenics are not
usually expected to take responsibility for others.

When, after several years in the group, she was married, she began to come
regularly. As she was now responsible for looking after her husband and home,
she could understand the meaning of responsibility towards the group. She also
needed the group and was able to make use of it better than before.

The cohesiveness of the group is made up of the reciprocal bonds between the
individual members and the group, and the members to one another.

Is the cohesiveness of the group a facilitating factor in therapy, or is it
mutative? For the individual member, it may be merely a precondition of change
(as Yalom 1981 found), though the sense of acceptance and support given by the
group may be vital to some distressed members. From the point of view of the
group, cohesiveness is vital for its existence. Bion (1961) distinguishes between
two kinds of bonds in the group: first, a basic, primitive potential for sticking
together, 'valency'; this is the basis for the 'basic assumption' defences, such as
fight or flight, pairing, dependency. Second, the conscious cooperation of the
'work group'.

I am not sure whether we ought to regard all the unconscious forces as
primitive, and whether all the positive forces are conscious ones. Primary process
is at the root of the 'free association' between group members. Also, the need to

understand and empathize with the other, to accept and help the other, seems to be intuitive and not necessarily the outcome of a rational decision.

CHAPTER 6

The Group and Perception

The way we perceive ourselves and others is subjective, individual and fundamental to the way we live. Our sense of our own identity is to some extent determined by the way we are perceived by others, and the way we see ourselves as being perceived by others.

Our interpretation of the actions of others determines how we act towards them. We interpret reality without realizing that we are doing so. Our interpretation, as far as we are concerned, is the reality.

This is true even at the basic level of sense perception: we 'hear' a train approaching, not a series of sounds which we interpret as those of an approaching train. We see a distant house on a hill, not a house which looks small and must therefore be distant. This immediacy of interpretation helps us to orient ourselves and makes the world comfortably familiar. Infants learn, early in life, to distinguish their mother and father from other persons, without being aware of the 'sense data' which lead them to do so.

The theory that we passively perceive sense data is no longer acceptable. The neurologist Oliver Sacks (1995) points out that we perceive the colours of objects as constant, though in fact the wavelength of light illuminating them differs under different conditions. He refers to Helmholtz, the physicist:

> There had to be some way, Helmholtz thought, of 'discounting the illumination' – and this he saw as 'unconscious inference' … Colour constancy, for him was a special example of the way in which we achieve perceptual constancy generally, make a subtle perceptual world from a chaotic sensory flux – a world which would not be possible if our perceptions were merely passive reflections of the unpredictable and inconstant input that bathes our receptors. (Sacks 1995, p.20)

The process of interpretation remains outside our awareness unless it goes wrong. Flying in a small plane over Elat, I was feasting my eyes on the close view of sand dunes and sea below us. Suddenly, the appearance of what looked like a toy ship and a toy house made me realize that we were not so close after all.

Optical 'illusions' teach us the immediacy of interpretation. Ernst Gombrich (1968) invites us to consider experimental illusions. The simplest of these is the view of three chairs, each seen through a peephole. When we look at these from the open side of the box, we find that only one is in fact a chair. One is a distorted structure and the third consists of unconnected parts. The reality we 'see' is not the reality at all. The peephole is the key to maintaining the illusion, as it holds us to one single viewpoint. As Bateson (1979) reminds us, we normally ascertain the nature of an object by scanning it with our eyes or moving around it.

We all more or less experience the same optical illusions. Consider more complex entities, like music. For some, music makes more sense than for others, for some Mozart does but not Bartok, European but not Indian music, or vice versa. It may be a matter of genetic disposition or training, but there is individual difference.

As one might expect, perception is even more subjective when it comes to persons. Imagine you have a friend called Jane, who is a teacher. She is perceived differently by each of her friends, by her pupils, her colleagues, by her husband and by her children. The way she perceives herself is different from all of these, though not unrelated. When Jane offers help to another, one person may consider this kind, another patronizing or intrusive. Consider Jack: to one person, he is a careful manager; to another, he is miserly. (Cf. R.D. Laing *et al.* 1965.)

It is in the nature of things that we are hardly aware of interpreting. It *is* reality we seem to perceive: Jane *is* patronizing, Jack *is* miserly. It is as if we saw the world through tinted spectacles and did not know we were wearing them. Various problems may arise from this. One is conflict through misunderstanding. If Jane means to be helpful, while a colleague regards her as interfering, neither may see the viewpoint of the other, and angry words may be exchanged. Misunderstandings of this nature occur even with those who know one another well, such as married couples. In fact, even more so, as each partner's belief that they 'know' the other inclines them to see or hear what they expected, and not what was actually done or said. It takes an outsider, such as a therapist (or therapeutic group), to show the individuals concerned that their perception is relative, that they are indeed wearing spectacles.

The certainty that our interpretation is the right one is a disadvantage. Flexibility is more useful than rigidity. Rigidity is a way of defining neurosis: it is not so much *how* neurotics perceive the world that is the trouble, it is the perseverance of their interpretation. Their spectacles will not come off. The problem of paranoids is of the same nature: the content of their thought would not matter so much, if only they could be sceptical about it. As a group member with obsessive thoughts said to another: 'You're talking rationally to me. But I'm not rational.'

Rigidity of perception often leads us to an impasse. It is as if we were trying to unlock a door, unsuccessfully, trying all our keys over and over again. It is only when we are able to stand back that we realize we have been at the wrong door all along.

We might define the aim of psychotherapy as bestowing the ability to take a different viewpoint, a fresh perspective. Bateson (1972[1964]) points to the shortcomings in merely changing the patient's perspective. The trouble is that the new, adaptive perception can become just as rigid as the old one. Moreover, it is liable to obsolescence when circumstances change. The other possibility is to facilitate change itself, to increase flexibility of perception.

To understand this better, let us consider two models: that of Gregory Bateson (1972[1935]), and that of Laing, Phillipson and Lee (1965).

Bateson's model

Gregory Bateson was briefly mentioned in Chapter 1. He distinguishes three levels of learning: Learning One, Learning Two, Learning Three. There is Zero Learning, which characterizes computers. A computer cannot learn from its mistakes as it makes none. (There is a moral in this for discouraged humans.)

Learning One is equivalent to Pavlovian conditioning. Even this is more complex than it seems, as Bateson realized when working with seals. Supposing a seal had been 'taught' a piece of behaviour, and the trainer wanted to demonstrate the process to students. The trainer would have to teach a new piece of behaviour, and this would confuse the seal. What was previously rewarded no longer is. After a while, the seal would grasp what was wanted: a new piece of behaviour for each run. The seal has learnt about responding to context. Bateson calls this Learning Two.

Learning Two is complex in human beings; people learn to respond differently in different contexts. There are 'context markers', such as the curtain going up on a play. We do not rush to help the character who falls down on the stage.

Bateson points out that no one is 'resourceful' or 'dependent' or 'generous' in a vacuum. 'Character traits' express themselves in an interpersonal context.

A person acquires his perception of contexts, his 'Learning Two', mostly early in infancy, and unconsciously. It is never negated by events, since it is not 'true' or 'false', but simply a way of perceiving context. Learning Two is self-validating, which explains its tendency not to change.

Let me illustrate this with a story. A patient has a blind friend who visits her regularly. She knows there is a table in the middle of the room and always walks round it. At one point my patient removed the table. Her visitor continued to avoid it, until it occurred to my patient to tell her it was no longer there. We are like the blind girl: we mentally walk around an obstacle we 'know' to be there, and continue to do so, thus never realizing it has gone.

Learning Three involves change in Learning Two (L2). We expect this to be difficult, but it can occur in psychotherapy or in religious conversion. Bateson points out that it involves more than replacing one kind of L2 by another: it means the facilitation of such replacement, that is, flexibility, the ability to unlearn and relearn about contexts.

Transference, according to Bateson, is an L2 phenomenon. The patient–therapist context is perceived as if it were one with a significant other from the past. Something of this nature occurs in all contexts. For example, a person may perceive all authority figures as invested with the characteristics of his father. What distinguishes transference in the therapeutic situation is that the analyst can observe its manifestations.

Learning Three is learning about Learning Two contexts. This could mean the acquisition of perspective. 'I see X as two different persons', or even 'I see X as threatening', rather than just acting on a conviction that he is so, means a gain in perspective. This is an aim of psychotherapy and, as we shall see, it occurs par excellence in the process of group psychotherapy.

As already mentioned, it is not enough to replace one kind of L2 by another, or to replace a 'maladaptive' way of looking at things by an 'adaptive' one. The aim is to acquire flexibility, the capacity for change itself.

The model of interpersonal perception

Laing and his co-workers (1965) drew attention to the importance of perception in human interaction. We do not respond to the other's behaviour, but to our interpretation of his behaviour.

Since our interpretation is necessarily subjective, actions may be perceived quite differently from the way they were intended by the agent. Thus, if I am upset, my friend may decide that the best way to help me is to remain calm. I might interpret this calm as insensitivity, and become even more upset. My friend thinks it is all the more important to remain calm, and I now suspect that he is deliberately trying to hurt me. There is thus a vicious spiral of misunderstanding and discord, anger may escalate, without any bad intention on anyone's part.

Laing, Phillipson and Lee (1965) list some qualities open to different interpretations:

- I act in a way that seems cautious to me, but cowardly to you.

- You regard yourself as courageous, I see you as foolhardy.

- He sees himself as friendly, she sees him as seductive.

- She sees herself as reserved, he sees her as haughty and aloof.

- She perceives herself as feminine, he perceives her as helpless and dependent.

- He sees himself as masculine, she sees him as overbearing and dominating.

It is evident that dyadic interaction is based on the way each person perceives the other, and how this accords with each person's perception of himself. Even the sense of one's own identity is related to the way one is perceived by others.

If I am unable to alter the other's experience of me, I can change my own experience of the other: this is done by projection. 'Projection refers to a mode of experiencing the other in which one experiences one's outer world in terms of one's inner world. Another way of putting this is that one experiences the perceptual world in terms of one's phantasy systems, without realizing that one is doing so' (Laing, Phillipson and Lee 1965, p.16–17).

Clearly, it is important how we think the other sees us. This is metaperspective. Joan may think she is quite a good mother; what worries her is that she thinks her husband thinks she is a bad mother.

Figures 6.1, 6.2, 6.3, 6.4, 6.5, 6.6, 6.7 and 6.8 are some examples of husband–wife perceptions. (The illustrations are my own.)

Figure 6.1 WW Wife's view of herself

Figure 6.2 HW Husband's view of wife

Figure 6.3 HH Husband's view of himself

Figure 6.4 WH Wife's view of husband

*Figure 6.5 HWW Husband's view of
how wife sees herself*

*Figure 6.6 WHH Wife's view of how husband
sees himself*

*Figure 6.7 HWH Husband's view of
how wife sees him*

*Figure 6.8 WHW Wife's view of how husband
sees her*

Each of these views refer to different aspects of oneself – general traits like being selfish or considerate, flexible or punctilious; traits in relation to others, such as being a good parent, a good organizer, and so on.

There is also meta-metaperspective. For instance, a wife may know (or believe) that her husband knows (or believes) that she sees herself as inadequate (WHWW).

She may know that he perceives her as inadequate, while she sees herself as efficient. (Her metaperspective of her husband's view of her differs from her self-perception.)

There can be concordance or discordance at any level. For example, a husband and wife may not realize that they actually agreed about the children; they may have thought they disagreed until this is clarified, perhaps in a therapy session. Conversely, they may disagree about an issue without realizing this. (All cases of discordance.) By understanding their differences, they can avoid conflict.

This paradigm applies to any dyadic relationship, and can easily be extended to relationships of more than two persons. Let us consider a special example singled out by Laing: understanding and feeling understood.

- Understanding: The way A sees B corresponds to the way B sees him/herself.

- Feeling understood: The way A thinks B sees him or her corresponds to the way A sees him/herself.

Being understood can be satisfying, although people vary in the extent to which they want to be understood. Being understood completely can be threatening to one's sense of self – be it by a parent or by a therapist.

Feeling persecuted may mean that people 'persist in attributing to the others a capacity to know what is going on in them far higher than the others actually possess… In intergroup and international relations as well as in interpersonal dyadic systems, the desire to be understood in some respects, the fears of being known in others…quite evidently play a large part' (Laing, Phillipson and Lee 1965, p.30).

The model of interpersonal perception shows how we can use here-and-now interpretations to enlarge perspective in the present. For example, if a man thinks people find him unlikeable, it may help if he can get feedback on what various people do think of him – as he well might in a therapy group. If, indeed, he evokes negative reactions through his behaviour, he can be helped to see this in a group. If a mother habitually fails to listen to what her daughter is saying, realizing what she does may help the mother. (This might happen in family therapy or in a thera-peutic group.) The historical origin of a perception need not necessarily be traced.

This is in line with modern trends of using transference in psychoanalysis. Rather than trying to discover what the analysand's actual relationship with his mother was in infancy, one works with the way he sees the analyst as mother in the transference.

There is an advantage in using 'here-and-now' rather than 'there-and-then' interpretations. A concentration on causes may bring about a sense of deter-minism. ('If what happened in childhood caused me to be what I am, how can I change?') I have found patients proud of knowing the causes of how they were now, as learnt in previous therapies. One patient expressed it in cybernetic terms: 'We have been programmed in certain ways.' Yalom (1980) also noted this tendency.

The therapeutic group has always been considered particularly suitable for here-and-now interpretation. The dimension of interpersonal space takes the place of the dimension of personal time; events take place in the interpersonal space of the group which reflect those in members' interpersonal space in their lives outside. Group members come to realize that they get themselves into the same sort of situations in the group as they do outside. They receive honest feedback about the reactions they evoke in others. What is more, multiple perspectives on these events are available; each group member has his or her own way of perceiving these events. This enables group members to compare their own perception of such events with the perceptions of others of these events.

Let us consider some ways in which the group enlarges the perspective of the individual member, and in what way this can facilitate flexibility and therapeutic change.

The role of the group in enlarging perspective

Perception of self

The individual member has a particular way of perceiving herself. She also has a view of how others see her (metaperception). She may or may not be satisfied with the way she thinks others see her. She may believe that others see her as better than she really is, or vice versa. Her self-esteem may be influenced by her metaperception of self. A self-fulfilling prophecy may be involved: others come to see her in the way she thinks (or fears) others see her.

> Ex. 6(i). Miss Y. was a solitary and diffident person who devalued herself. In the group she spoke little at first. She never volunteered an opinion on the problems of others. In the course of time, she changed: she began to look better, live differently. She told the group: 'I need to be told again and again that my opinion is valued. At home, I was regarded as stupid. No one wanted to listen to me.'

> Ex. 6(ii). Eric confided to a couples group that people considered him square and sexless and devoid of humour (or so he thought). A woman in the group said this was not the impression he made at all, and another confirmed it.

Often the diffident group member finds it easier to talk about others than about himself.

> Ex. 6(iii). Daryl, a depressed carpenter, did not want to trouble the group whenever he was asked about himself. Nor did he immediately accede to requests to express his opinion in general. One day he was drawn into helping Dorothy, a new member, who was a librarian. For a space of time he was therapist. His new capability encouraged him, and he gradually became more involved in the group.

Sometimes we find that feedback from the group on their various perceptions has a noticeable effect on a member over a period of time. Let us follow the group process in a median group (twenty members) over a period of three meetings, with special reference to Stephen. Stephen was a single man in his forties with the characteristics of a schizoid personality.

Ex. 6(iv). Stephen had not spoken since I joined the group about six weeks ago. The first time I heard him speak was when Robin, the junior co-therapist, announced that he was going to leave. Stephen remarked: 'I am in a terrible transference situation with Patrick' (Patrick de Maré, the senior therapist). 'I may be forced to leave. It's even countertransference.' Asked what he meant, he replied that Pat did not like him. De Maré remarked that Stephen was putting him up as a straw man, being afraid of taking on the group. A group member asked Stephen why he had not discussed this before; he might have found the group was on his side. Stephen now accused the therapist of waffling. One group member agreed; another apologized that her eyelids were drooping. Someone asked Stephen how the prospect of Robin's leaving was affecting him. He admitted that it affected him very much.

In the following meeting Stephen told the group that his neighbour seemed disturbed. He had told her to go and seek help, but he feared that this might have driven her to take all her tablets. Several group members reassured him; he had done all he could. Robin linked his words to what had earlier been said about the future of the group: replying to questions who would replace Robin, Patrick had suggested that group members take it in turn to be co-convenors. Robin thought that Stephen was telling this story to ensure that he would not be a co-convenor, as he believed he was damaging the group. The group retorted that he was not damaging. Robin replied that this was how he perceived himself. I ventured that Stephen had merely been expressing doubt about himself.

It is probable that the supportive attitude of the group in the previous session had encouraged Stephen to speak up in this one. In the following session we heard him again.

Vanessa, a psychologist, described the difficulty of leading large groups; her own experience was of groups of teachers. The worst part was people not turning up. Shaun, a clergyman, described similar problems with church groups. Some group members wondered why it was easy to talk in pubs. Cynthia remarked that this was really talking in twos and threes rather than in groups.

Stephen said he couldn't talk in the church group, he was afraid of drying up. He would rather just be there. But he found himself talking to an old lady at the bus stop; she told him her life history. 'Why do I do that?' 'Because you can get off,' said the therapist. 'Why do they choose me? With that face of mine… I look at myself in the mirror in the morning and I want to kill what I see there.' 'You can see hate,' said de Maré.

Members asked de Maré if he had said that the group was a mirror. He had not, but some members thought that it was. Diana told Stephen that in her view he had a nice face. 'If I saw you in the street I'd go and speak to you, if I dared.' Someone asked Stephen if that frightened him. He said it did. Why? Because it made him think of love. And why was that frightening? Because it meant having to feel concern for another person.

I remarked that the group was indeed a mirror, in the sense that members reflected back the way they saw you. Someone said that Stephen saw someone else hating him. Stephen said this might be so, but he could not unscramble it. 'The group will unscramble it for you,' said de Maré.

We note that Stephen had brought himself for treatment, a new venture for him. The group responded. Later in the same meeting, Stephen made a bid for symmetry. He wanted to be helper as well as helped.

This is what happened. Shaun says there is no equality, and is asked what he means. 'In society...in a group.' Stephen responds: 'The fact that you have doubts does not make you a worse priest.' Shaun reflects on doubt, and mentions Father Huddleston, who is said to have loved everyone. The group discusses this: is it possible to love everyone?

I remarked that we had been talking about two kinds of groups, charismatic leader groups and groups like ours in which everyone helped everyone else, the leader exercising a kind of negative capability, empowering the group to work. When Stephen talked about Shaun being a good priest in spite of doubts, he was also saying something about himself. Though he had doubts, has his own problems, this ought not to prevent him from helping others.

Stephen said this was the first time the group had given him something. He clearly found these sessions helpful.

We can see in this segment of the group process how the feedback of the group on how they saw Stephen, together with its warm concern, changed his self-concept sufficiently to make it possible for him to become both 'patient' and 'therapist' in the group. Originally he had believed himself unable to participate at all, being in what he described as a state of 'bad transference'. He expected little from the group; he probably thought they would reject him if they knew the depth of his self-hate and despair. They proved him wrong. They cared for him enough to support him, going so far as to back him up when he attacked the convenor. (They assumed that the latter was strong enough to take it.)

In the following meeting Stephen brought up the question of his ability to help people in outside life. Robin's comment on his reporting destructiveness accorded with only one side of the picture. Stephen expressed doubt, and needed confirmation by the group that he was constructive. His receiving it had a beneficial effect.

In the last of the meetings described Stephen took part in the dialogue on the difficulty of speaking up in social groups, which no doubt also referred to his difficulty in speaking in the median group. He went on to the question of whether he was likeable or hateable (the lady at the bus stop, his view of himself in the mirror). It must have taken a good deal of trust in the group to raise this. After it had been sensitively and empathically dealt with, he wondered if he could be a full member of the group, which meant being both helper and helped: Shaun, he thought, was not a worse priest for having doubts; meaning that he, Stephen, could still be a good therapist while having problems of his own.

Symmetry is an important feature of the group-analytic group. Every member is both helper and helped, therapist and needy member. In life, most mature persons have a need for symmetry: they want to give as well as receive; they need to be needed. When those whose need is great, like the recently bereaved, refrain from calling on friends, one reason is the fear that they will inevitably receive more than they can give.

The human need for symmetry is sometimes forgotten by therapists; for example, in the case of hospitalized patients. They need the experience of being useful to others as soon as the acute phase of their illness is over.

Seeking to have others see us as we want to be seen

As Laing, Phillipson and Lee (1965) pointed out, much of our activity is aimed at trying to get others to see us as we want to be seen. We may selectively seek out those who can do so. In the therapeutic group this is impossible, as the selection is not made by the members. The group member therefore has to work with the given others.

Stephen brought his 'helping self' to the group, to affirm to himself that there was such an aspect of him. (The therapist's interpretation that he was destructive may have acted as a challenge.) He also brought the 'hating self', not because he wanted this confirmed or denied, but evidently to explore whether he was acceptable in spite of this trait.

Members may spend a good deal of energy promoting the self-image they want to project, particularly in a new group. Often the 'helper' image is preferred; it is difficult to let the group see one's neediness, except in the case of very immature or psychotic patients. Thus, potential 'therapists' may dominate and compete for pride of place in any group, and not only in groups of professionals.

Guntrip (1968) emphasizes the difficulty of exposing one's needy self, describing it as the most difficult and ultimate step in individual therapy. What is helpful in the group is the example of others: this makes it easier, for many, to follow suit.

Ex. 6(v). In a slow-open group, Celia had been talking about her relationship with her mother. She had described the ways in which her mother had made her feel insignificant as a child, such as not responding to her questions. Now her mother was visiting from abroad. After an argument Celia had told her to leave the house; she felt bad about this. Felix, who was attending for the first time, began to talk about his father, dead for ten years. 'Five years after he was dead, my feelings for him changed. I realized I hated him... I don't know why I'm talking about this, it's my first time here.'

Ex. 6(vi). Martha's father had sexually abused her in childhood. In her late twenties, she had been referred to me for individual therapy. I invited her to join the group. Neither she nor I believed that she would be able to talk about the incest in the group. Indeed, she joined the group after a great deal of hesitation, and spoke little at first. At one point Frank asked her whether she had undergone some sexual trauma in childhood (without explicitly recalling his own). She answered in the affirmative, and suddenly found it natural to talk about her own bad experience.

Seeing oneself and being seen: inside and outside the group

We can observe only the events which occur in the group. When a group member describes how people outside the group see him, this is not open to observation; it is his own metaperspective. It can, however, be compared with what happens in the group.

One's self-image may be better or worse than it is actually perceived by the group. A man who told the group that people saw him as devoid of humour was told by the group that here he was perceived otherwise. Conversely, a schizophrenic woman was surprised to be told by the group that she appeared unfriendly. She had been behaving according to her own rules, with no regard for reciprocity or social conventions. Yet she would ask the group why she had no friends.

Ex. 6(vii). Helen, an unmarried woman in her thirties, had 'grown up' in the group. From staying at home with her parents, doing nothing, she had advanced to moving in with her sister (in another town), whom she helped with her children. She was now working in a sheltered workshop. In the group, she had graduated from being silent, sometimes even turning her back on the group, to intelligent participation. Her comments on the problems of others were often very perceptive.

In one meeting, the group asked why she did not wait with the others in the waiting room, and why she did not greet the others. 'Why should I greet you if I do not want to?' Yet she complained that her workmates seemed not to like her, nor agree to make friends with her. The group pointed out that her behaviour was experienced as unfriendly. Dennis said he understood Helen was sick, but others might regard her as 'stuck up'. Sidney said he was hurt when Helen did not say hallo, as did Jessica. Helen seemed to accept this (although she continued not to greet group members).

The therapeutic group is not a social group and acceptance by it is not an end in itself – a pitfall with some cult groups, or groups which turn into cults. It is a bridge for enabling members to make relationships outside. Zinkin (1997) holds that, on the contrary, acceptance by the group is sufficiently different to unfit members from finding acceptance outside. One may hope, however, that the group member can gain confidence in the group, can try out new ways of relating, and learn from the feedback given him by the group.

CHAPTER 7

The View from Different Perspectives

As the group is itself the agent of therapy in group analysis, the therapist's main task is to enable and empower it to do its work. Foulkes (1948) had faith in the ability of the group to observe and make interpretations. 'The therapist in an individual situation has to make these contributions, for example interpretations, and voice them in his own words. The group conductor's aim is to let this come from the group' (Foulkes, 1948, p.136). The main job is thus to create the conditions which make this possible. 'The Conductor wants to use the group as an instrument for therapy. By maintaining the group-analytic situation, he forges this instrument and he continues refining it' (Foulkes 1948, p.135).

To enable us to do so, it is a good thing to understand the perspectives of group members, of the group as a whole, and of the conductor. What can be observed by whom? Are there aspects of the group observable only by the therapist? What observations can usefully be made by the group? Let us look at a map of perspectives of the group.

Perspectives of the individual member

We shall consider five perspectives of the individual member (IM):

- IMs on him/herself
- IM on another IM
- IM on interaction between other IMs
- IM on the group as a whole
- IM on the therapist.

The individual member's perspective on him/herself

Each individual has a perspective on herself, of who and what she is. As a group member, one concern may be how she is seen by others. She has a metaperspective, a view of how she is perceived by others. Some believe that others see them as worse than they really are, some the reverse. Some hold that others view them realistically.

Group members learn about themselves in two ways. First, they may see themselves in a new light through their experience in the group. Second, the group acts as a mirror, reflecting how they appear in relating to others.

The group can have a perspective on the IM which enables it to make a mutative interpretation. It can make the perceived group member aware of short-comings or, conversely, better his own view of himself. Of course, the therapist could give this kind of feedback. This would, however, short-circuit the group process. Besides, feedback coming from the group is usually more effective than feedback coming from the therapist. He is perceived as the embodiment of authority, while the group member is 'one of us'. When it is a matter of correcting faults, the IM might rebel. When it is a matter of a more positive view than members have of themselves, it is, after all, the therapist's job to be accepting. In the group, acceptance has to be earned.

Another reason for the importance of feedback from the group is that the group perspective is not uniform; each group member has his own view. This avoids polarization into black and white, and the tendency to defend one's viewpoint against someone who opposes it. The realization that there are many ways of perceiving a thing helps the group member understand that his own per-spective is but one of many.

The individual member's perspective on other members

Each group member has a view of every other member. This view is coloured by her own personality, her own projections and identifications. For example, a group member may be sensitive to a quality in another which she herself possesses and fails to recognize in herself. The IM is thus perceived from a range of perspectives, as wide as the number of members in the group.

Zinkin (1983, p.115) writes: 'Group therapy reduces the tendency to regard the therapist's view as objectively correct because the presence of the other group members introduces several other views… Insight is better thought of as a signifi-cantly new view of the self rather than the acquiring of objective new knowledge.' He also speaks of 'malignant mirroring', produced by the horror of seeing oneself in a mirror, which sometimes occurs when another group member resembles oneself.

The IM reveals himself in the group through his mode of relating to others. What he does in the group gives direct information, open to scrutiny here-and-now, whereas his narrative about his life is filtered through his own spectacles, as it were. This direct, here-and-now information is unique to the group setting. It makes for the possibility of feedback from any other IM, from the group as a whole, and from the therapist if necessary.

The here-and-now clarification in the group corresponds to a certain type of transference interpretation in individual therapy. The therapist makes observations on the patient's behaviour, as reflected in his behaviour towards her. This can be difficult, as she is both the object of transference and its observer. In the therapeutic group the IM tends to behave as he does in his life outside, or as he did towards significant others. The group can be said to be the object of transference. Yet it has space enough to be observer too.

Group members can compare the life narrative of an IM with his mode of relating to the group. One man talked about girls always refusing his second invitation. 'Perhaps you don't show enough interest in them – this is what happens in the group. You don't seem to be interested in other people.'

The IM's perspective on another IM is coloured by his personality and experience. There is no such thing as an objective view. Indeed, the value of the situation lies in the variety of perspectives available to each IM. It is the multiplicity of views in evidence which may help the IM to step back from his own narrow perspective, and see his view as just one of many possible ones.

Unconscious elements enter into the IM's perception of another to a greater or lesser degree. It is usually held that the transference of group members to one another is a sibling one, but it may take any form.

> Ex. 7(i). In one group, Sheila and Donald found themselves, more than once, incomprehensively quarrelling. Sheila was a married woman with two teenage children, Donald was a single man of 22. It occurred to Sheila that she saw in Donald her teenage son, while Donald soon realized that she represented his mother.

The individual member's perspective on interaction between other members

Group members (GMs) are usually quite adept at perceiving the nature of the interaction between other GMs.

> Ex. 7(ii). Gerald was a newcomer to the group. In the course of one session, Sheila told him all sorts of things about her relationship to her husband. After some fifteen minutes, Vivienne remarked: 'But we've heard all this before.' 'He hasn't,' said Sheila. 'But we can't give him a résumé of the whole group,' retorted Vivienne. The therapist pointed out that Vivienne was right; the two were excluding the rest of the group.

Vivienne had in fact noted an instance of pairing, with which the group colluded. As Bion (1961) points out, they apparently hope that the Messiah might thus be conceived.

The individual member's perspective on the group as a whole

Sometimes a group member is able to step back and observe what is happening in the group as a whole. This is uncommon; the therapist is in a better position to observe the whole group.

> Ex. 7(iii). In a couples group, people were vociferous about the shortcomings of their spouses. Unexpectedly, a rather quiet man pointed to the problem: 'We are all complaining about our partners, wanting them to be what they are not, instead of looking what is wrong with us. We are not really working as a group.' The group proceeded to explore this issue.

The individual member's perspective on the therapist

Each individual member has a perspective on the therapist(s), perceiving both his real and fantasized qualities. Much of this is not verbally expressed, at least not directly. Positive transference to the therapist(s) can be useful initially in building the new member's first link to the group. On the other hand, if the therapist encourages individual relating to her, rather than to the group, this hinders the development of the group matrix.

Transference perceptions are, as one might expect, highly tinged with emotion: Perceiving the therapist as all-powerful and benevolent, and feeling dependent, expecting comfort in one's distress and solutions to one's problems, as if one were an infant looking to one's mother for such help. Perceiving the therapist as powerful but harsh; being afraid of her. Feeling jealousy, wishing to be special; perceiving the therapist as regarding one as special.

As transference perceptions and feelings are not often communicated overtly, the trainee therapist can best learn about them through participation in a group. I recall how I, as an experienced therapist, took part in a median group over a year, and found myself wanting to be special. (The group was both for students and patients, in about equal proportions.) This was against all my principles, and I knew it was wrong, but I felt a need to talk to the therapist, after the group; I helped him by writing summaries and sending them to him. When the co-therapist was about to leave, and the principal therapist suggested group members as possible co-covenors, I was disappointed when he did not suggest me – despite my awareness of the fact that I was leaving London at the end of the year.

Transference to the therapist may express itself in various indirect ways. For example, if the therapist is a physician, the group member may express himself in somatic terms, in terms of symptoms, in order to invite a response from the therapist rather than the group. (This is particularly the case with psychotic or psychosomatic patients.) The best way to deal with this is to ask the group member to translate this into interpersonal language: what has happened to him, and how does he feel about it?

Metaperspective

A metaperspective is a perspective on a perspective. For example, how Jack thinks his employer perceives him; how Jane thinks her friends perceive her. The group gives an opportunity to individuals for checking on metaperspectives. If Marilyn believes that the group considers her conceited, she can receive feedback from the group. If David believes that people regard him as devoid of humour, this can be checked too; the group may be considered a microcosm (to use Yalom's term): people evoke much the same reaction in the group as they do in the world outside.

The group can thus function as a workshop for comparing one's metaperspective with the perspectives others have on oneself. In social settings this would be difficult or impossible.

Perspectives of the group

Let us consider four perspectives of the group:

- The group on itself
- The group on the IM
- The group on the interaction between IMs
- The group on the therapist.

The group's perspective on itself

By the nature of things, the therapist has a better perspective on the group than the group has on itself. It is nonetheless a good thing to encourage the group to observe itself, monitor itself, and take responsibility for the group process.

In the vignette of the couples group (Ex. 7(iii)) a group member noticed that the group had fallen into a rut of finding fault with their spouses, instead of really working.

Another instance occurred in a median group. A group member pointed out that they were always criticizing A for 'waffling', whereas B did the same thing and was always allowed to get away with it.

I have given Ex. 7(iii) as one of an individual member's having perspective on the group. It could be understood as the group having a perspective on itself. It is a moot point whether to take the instances above as examples of the IM's perspective on the group, or of the whole group's perspective on itself. If the rest of the group readily agrees with the first spokesperson, it is probably true to say that she had been representing the view of the whole group.

In each case one individual member makes the observation; perhaps this one member has distanced himself from the group and seen things differently. Should we then regard these as instances of the individuals' perspective on the group, rather than the group's perspective on itself? I think it depends whether the rest of the group is able to see the group in the light of this new perspective. Group members cannot, after all, speak all at once – at least, one hopes they would not.

The group may see a life situation reiterated in the group; de Maré (personal communication) calls this 'transposition'.

> Ex. 7(iv). In a meeting of a median group, Marion complained that her mother had never listened to her when she was a child. Finding the group attentive, she expressed gratitude: now she was being listened to.

The group's perspective on the individual member

The group has a perspective on the individual member. It is by dint of being part of the group that the IM feels empowered to take a look at another IM, to be inquisitive about her private life, to be critical and presume to interpret her motives. In the same capacity, she undertakes to be tolerant, sympathetic and caring. As an individual it might not be acceptable to be as curious, as critical or as affectionate.

The individual member has a view of how she is seen by the group: this is her metaperspective. She has internalized the group as a whole. She is usually less preoccupied by the views of individual members.

The concept of group perspective does not imply a unitary view. Group members have viewpoints as diverse as their personalities, and in that lies the strength of the group. Group members often take different roles: if one has been critical, another may find himself wanting to be supporting to compensate. If the group finds itself drawn to go in one direction, this could sometimes signal the beginning of a destructive process, such as scapegoating.

The group's communication of its perspective on the IM usually makes up a significant part of group interaction. The group could thus treat a needy member for the major part of the session.

> Ex. 7(v). Martha had joined the group recently and for four sessions was unable to speak. Even simple everyday questions seemed unanswerable. This time she had made up her mind to speak up. 'I have a problem. I'm chronically late for work. When it gets bad, my boss threatens to sack me, then I come on time for a while. Now it's getting bad again.' The group rallied to her help, relieved that she had at last been able to talk. Someone suggested alarm clocks. 'It goes deeper than that,' said Martha. Frank asked about her childhood, and Martha spoke of a harsh mother who had shown her no love.

At present Martha was living with an old woman who was very nervous and often shouted at her. 'I seem to be addicted to suffering.' The group asked why she did not live with a girl her own age. 'Well, I tried once...' Erica remarked: 'They say that people who get up late don't respect themselves.' Martha replied that she did not esteem herself highly. Her family had treated her as an inferior being. Her two brothers had been treated quite differently, they had received every encouragement.

Here the whole group was exploring Martha's problem, drawing her out through support and interest. Frank's question and Erica's remark had advanced the process.

Ex. 7(vi). In a group of psychotic outpatients, there was one couple: Daniel had married in the course of his group therapy, and his wife Deborah had joined later at her request. They have one daughter (aged 5 at the time of session described).

In a later session, Bernie remarked to Deborah: 'You always talk about problems you have with your little girl, never about difficulties between Daniel and yourself. It seems to be easier to talk about the child.'

Group members expressed agreement. Deborah at once brought what was ostensibly a marital problem: Daniel had revealed to his parents that they were going out to dinner. She did not think he ought to disclose such intimate details. The group did not know what she was talking about.

I commented that Deborah seemed to be telling us that she could not discuss marital problems with the group. She repeated her accusation. 'Who makes the decisions in your family?' I asked. For the first time Daniel spoke up: 'Deborah is rather dominant.'

Bernie had made a valid point; Deborah did almost constantly talk about the child. Moreover, she behaved as if she were the only significant parent. When asked why she did not enlist Daniel's help, she once said: 'He is more sick than I. He takes strong medication.'

Daniel accepted the passive role assigned to him by Deborah. This is in contrast to the role of adviser and guru that he had played in the group before he was married (and still did to some extent). As Bernie rightly pointed out, the couple rarely discussed the relationship between them.

The group's perspective on the interaction between individual members

The group as a whole can often observe the interaction between two group members. They may remark that one IM is offending another, or expressing envy of another, or not giving another IM a chance to speak.

The group's perspective on the therapist

The group has a perspective on the therapist, both as he or she really is and in their fantasy, in the transference. As to their view of the real therapist, the group therapist is more transparent, less opaque, than the individual therapist: this may be because she is seen from several angles. When the therapist addresses one group member, or addresses the group through him, other less involved group members have a relatively detached view. Her real qualities are perceived: she may be seen as motherly, perhaps overprotective, or as aloof, controlling or enabling.

On the other hand, there is a good deal of fantasy, of transference, in the group's perception of the therapist. As we might expect, it largely remains latent until the occasion arises for expression.

> Ex. 7(vii). John, who had been my co-therapist conducting a group of psychotic outpatients, had suddenly decided to leave after his wife had given birth to their second son. He had been with the group for five years. For some reason, he refused to return to tell the group he was leaving. Much as I tried, explaining what this would do to the group's sense of trust, I could neither understand nor persuade him.
>
> The group expressed anger, surprise and similar feelings for several sessions. One couple threatened to leave for apparently unrelated reasons and I did my best to rebuild confidence.
>
> Three months later, a silent student observer was about to leave after ten months. On announcing her leaving, the group at once compared her to John. 'Not like John, who never said goodbye... How could he do such a thing to us... after all this time... We wish you success... Is anyone going to come in your place?'
>
> Although she had been silent, the observer had clearly been perceived as a co-therapist in the transference. Her presence had been important to the group. Perhaps simply being heard was important to the group. This, incidentally, was a spontaneous expression of transference needing no interpretation.

The therapist's perception of transference, and what he or she does with it, belongs to the next section.

Therapist's perspectives

We shall first consider four perspectives of the therapist. Later we consider the therapist's metaperspectives.

- Therapist on IM (including the intrapsychic)
- Therapist on intra-group relating (one member to another, one member to the group)
- Therapist on group as a whole

- Therapist on group's relating to therapist.

The therapist's perspective on group's relating to therapist

There are non-transference aspects of the group's relating to the therapist. They deserve the therapist's attention. For example, what are the group's expectations of the therapist? They may be difficult to discern when a group is new, easier later in its life.

Another matter is the group's feelings towards the therapist in the here-and-now situation. Does the group appear to be satisfied, complacent, envious, angry? It is perhaps protecting the therapist from a group member's aggression? In one meeting of a couples group, one of the men became extremely aggressive, fortunately only verbally. The group proceeded to defend and protect the therapist pair.

The therapist may or may not wish to share his observations with the group. In one case, a therapist about to go on holiday wondered aloud if the group was angry. 'I envy you', said one group member. It was important to make it possible to express this feeling.

The therapist's perspective on the individual member

The therapist certainly has a unique perspective on the individual member and the way the latter manages his own life. He may have previous acquaintance with the group member. He has a special knowledge of psychopathology. He may have had a good deal of experience in individual therapy, and it may be second nature to him to make individual interpretations.

It is very tempting to make use of this as a first reaction, which means to engage in individual therapy with the group as background. To do so, however, blocks the development of the group's therapeutic capability. The message is that only the therapist/conductor can 'treat' group members. Dependence is fostered. The bond between therapist and IM is strengthened, making for a leader-centred group.

The therapist may very actively observe and think in terms of individual as well as group interpretations. Mostly, it is best to sit back and allow the group to use its intuition and understanding of the individual member in the first instance. This will preserve the group-centred nature of the group.

The therapist's perspective on intra-group relating

While the group can clearly observe the IM in the group space, its view of interaction between IMs is less clear, it tends to be involved. The therapist has a particularly good perspective on intra-group relating, being relatively detached. The IM relating to another IM, the IM relating to the whole group, make important material for interpretation. It may throw light on the IMs relating to significant persons outside the group.

Here, too, it is best to give a chance to the group to make its observation first. It might be encouraged to do so. When S. had been relating her woes at length, in a whining and helpless manner, I asked the group how this made them feel. In this case, the group's response was far more effective than any interpretation I could make as a therapist.

> Ex. 7(viii). In a group of psychotic outpatients, Peter arrived one day, telling the group he had decided he wanted sheltered housing. Would the therapist help him? Would she write a letter? Could she write it today? He took up a lot of time and silenced other members who wanted to speak. He claimed that his financial difficulties and high rent made him feel pressured. Shira said others, too, had to cope with pressures. 'But you have a partner, and you have sex with him.' Shira appeared hurt; she retorted that this had nothing to do with it.
>
> Peter interrupted other members who wanted to speak, asking for reassurance. Bernie repeated that others had been in need, yet had not behaved like this. The therapist invited Peter to look at what he was doing to the group. It could well be that he used the same tactics with his parents, thus putting their backs up.
>
> Daniel said that one ought to ask for things politely. Peter reiterated that he was under pressure. Deborah reported an instance when she had arrived at a place very thirsty, yet had asked very politely for water, much as she was in need of it.
>
> Peter took up quite a lot of group time, but eventually calmed down.

When the therapist observes the IMs relating to the group, reciprocity has to be taken into account.

> Ex. 7(ix). In a group of neurotics, Martha often found it difficult to talk. When she did, she made it clear that her problems were deep and painful. The group came to feel dwarfed by their enormity, believing that their own problems were trivial in comparison. When she had difficulty in beginning to speak, the group was frozen, waiting for her, unable to talk about anything else.
>
> I pointed out that she was undoubtedly distressed, but was also holding the whole group to ransom in her silences. The group had a part in this, too: they felt their difficulties were minor in comparison to hers, and allowed the group to freeze.

The therapist's perspective on the group as a whole

The therapist has a perspective on the group as a whole, which is more or less unique. The group may, on occasion, glimpse and understand itself, but it lacks this view from the outside. It is important for the therapist to keep this perspective in view. He is like a painter who half closes his eyes in order to take in the landscape as a whole, rather than get absorbed in a detail, a single object in the landscape. It does take a shift of perspective to stop worrying about a specific group member, and consider what is happening to the whole group.

Whether or not to share these observations with the group is the next consideration. The first rule is to be discriminating in one's observations. When a group member makes a point, it does not necessarily mean that he is speaking for the whole group: it is too facile to translate this into 'the group is saying...'

> Ex. 7(x). In a ward meeting in a therapeutic community, Vera complained about the food, and then asked how she could get to the dentist. A staff member interpreted that the group was complaining that the staff was not giving them enough. Even without knowing the group or Vera, it is clear that this is not necessarily true. Only one group member had spoken. In fact, Vera was making one of her pleas for monopolizing attention, and was not giving the rest of the group a chance to express themselves. The right intervention, therefore, would have been to point this out and open the dialogue to the group.

The misuse of 'voice of the group' interpretations, as in Ex. 7(x), is often resented by group members who think differently and possibly had no chance to express their views. When relevant, it is useful to describe differences: 'Some members of the group think X, others think Y'. This kind of intervention legitimizes difference.

Observations on the group as a whole may be divided into content and process perceptions.

CONTENT PERCEPTIONS

Foulkes (1948) observed that free-floating dialogue in the group is the equivalent of free association. This implies that apparently unconnected remarks may have common roots, a common underlying theme. If the therapist can point to this common theme when it is not obvious, this can open up communication.

I have used content interpretations to sum up a group session which, on the face of it, seemed unsatisfactory.

> Ex. 7(xi). In a group of psychotic outpatients, Helen, married for less than a year, wondered about the right way to divide her time between her husband and her ageing parents (with whom she had spent much time before). She spoke about adopting a child (although she knew she would not be able to take care of him). Deborah spoke of conflicting advice about bringing up her daughter. Daniel expressed concerns about his religious practices. Group members seemed unable to relate to one another.

> I said that the group dialogue reminded me of a traditional story, told by S.Y. Agnon, about a man who lost himself in the wood and could not find his way out. After three days he met another man and was very relieved. 'Now I shall find

my way out.' To his disappointment, the second man said he too was lost. 'We shall have to find a new way together.'

Paul remarked that the group, too, seemed to be lost in the wood. They would find a way out together.

PROCESS PERCEPTIONS

It is important to look at the group process. If the group is working well, there is no need to intervene. Interpretations are superfluous if they are merely right, but have no function. When the group process is stuck, or beginning to be destructive, it is up to the therapist to make the right intervention to bring about change.

It may be quite difficult to find the right intervention when the group has embarked on an aggressive course, or one member is being uncontrollably aggressive, or is monopolizing the group. One answer is to identify the trend at an early stage.

Here is an example of a mildly destructive segment of process interpreted.

Ex. 7(xii). Some time before Helen was to be married, she voiced her concerns about married life and her new role. Group members made various comforting remarks, telling her it would be all right. I pointed out that the group was not giving Helen a chance to discuss her worries, which were quite natural.

Metaperspectives of the therapist

The therapist may find it useful to comment on the way an IM perceives him/herself and compare this with the way he or she is perceived by the group.

- Therapist on IM's self-perception
- Therapist on IM's perception of therapist (on individual transference)
- Therapist on group's perception of therapist (on group transference)
- Therapist on his or her perception of the group (awareness of countertransference).

The therapist's perception of individual member's perception of the therapist (including individual transference)

The IM's relating to the therapist is one aspect of group events of which the therapist is probably well aware.

The question is whether it is important to focus on it in the light of the group process. The therapist has to decide whether to concentrate on it or ignore it.

A time to interpret individual transference is when it impedes progress in the group. For example, a group member may look to the therapist as an omnipotent helper, making repeated demands, while the rest of the group is on another tack.

The therapist's perception of the group's perception of the therapist (including group transference)

Transference of the group to the therapist, or therapists, is always present. The question is how often and when it requires interpretation.

As already mentioned, the transference interpretation does not have the same crucial role in group psychotherapy as it has in individual therapy. In the latter, it is a here-and-now interpretation, the only one there is. The patient transfers modes of relating to significant persons to the therapeutic situation.

In the group, the GM relates to the group much as he does (or did) to significant others in life. But here we can make here-and-now interpretations on the way the GM relates to the group. His relating to the therapist, or the group's relating to the therapist, is less important than in dyadic therapy.

Oblique allusions to transference feelings may be worth interpreting. For example, when group members talk about inadequate treatment by their family doctors, or no longer trusting them, one may make a transference interpretation: perhaps they are feeling this way about the group therapist. Manifestations of transference are looked for in obvious situations, an impending holiday, a therapist leaving or having left.

Sometimes transference manifestations are quite subtle and not easily recognized.

> Ex. 7(xiii). In a group of neurotics, one meeting was opened by Graham apologizing for his absence last week; he had worked out of town and had been held up at the last moment. He failed to get through to any of us to let us know. My co-therapist reminded him of the rules rather sternly. This seemed to paralyse the group for several minutes. Then Frank brought some good news about himself: he, who had always considered himself responsible for the family budget, and suffered from this, had managed to involve his wife. He felt pleased and liberated.
>
> There were some responses, then the dialogue dried up once more. Graham broke the silence. His father's 'authoritarian' manner had always put his back up. 'Does this relate to me?' asked Frank. 'No, it was just in my head.'
>
> Realizing that there was something wrong, I decided to intervene: 'I wonder why we are talking about authoritarian parents. It might be something to do with the group's relationship with the therapists. Perhaps we are too authoritarian.' 'Not at all,' someone retorted.
>
> A new member now brought up a subject which had troubled him, and everyone joined in the dialogue. Whatever had tied down the group seemed to have gone.
>
> In the discussion after the group, my co-therapist pointed out that the group had not got going, but after some intervention of mine it went well. She did not understand why. I argued that early interventions by the therapists tended to set

the tone, and could paralyse the group's spontaneous associations. It could be that she had been too stern in reminding Graham of the rules. She concluded that Graham had probably referred to her when he spoke of his authoritarian father, even if he was unaware of the connection. I was glad of her observations on the group process, as I was not sufficiently detached to judge the effect of my interpretations.

What are the indications for interpreting transference to the therapist? When it seems to disrupt the group process, it may be necessary to do so. The group may need to be made aware of disturbing feelings which are expressed only in hints. Feelings about someone's forthcoming holidays are one example, the imminent or recent leaving of a co-therapist is another.

Another consideration is the relative importance, at that point in the group process, of the real relationship described. To make a transference interpretation blocks further exploration of the real relationship.

> Ex. 7(xiv). In a couples group, Tessa had always taken the role of therapist and never revealed her own problems. After a year, she began to describe her painful relations with her mother in childhood. We considered this was important for her, and a gateway to her adopting the patient role. There was a transference aspect (she also had difficulties in her relationship with me), but to have inter-preted it then would have inhibited this process.

There are theories according to which every communication of the group is inter-preted as transference to the therapist. To do so is to treat the group as one single unit, taking no account of interpersonal processes within the group. It is also to deny the validities of references to the real world.

A sad example of the destruction that can thus be wrought is what happened in a London therapeutic community day hospital, as documented by Claire Baron (1987). A director was appointed who worked on the model described above. When the day patients complained that the place was dirty, this was interpreted as referring to psychic dirt within. All groups had eventually to be conducted in conformity with the model. This led to the deterioration and closure of the thera-peutic community.

In all cases, it is important for the therapist to switch perspectives between reality and transference aspects, and to consider whether a transference interpreta-tion would facilitate or be destructive to the therapeutic process.

The therapist's perception of his or her perception of the group (awareness countertransference)

It is always important for the group therapist to be aware of countertransference. Is she favouring a particular group member, or disliking another? What feelings arise from the group process, and could they be influencing her relating to the group?

The presence of a co-therapist is often helpful in pointing out some manifestations of countertransference, particularly when they arise from feelings towards particular group members.

There is a type of countertransference which is a projection of the unconscious of the patient (see Searles 1965) and this can be very useful. The group may be communicating a sense of hope or despair without this being evident from their words. For the therapist to say so may open up communication in this direction.

CHAPTER 8

The Person of the Therapist

Science, Art and Intuition

This book has so far gone from the abstract to the concrete, from the more theoretical to the more practical. After mapping out the terrain (Chapter 7), it might have made sense to write a guide on how to go. But it did not work; the chapter grew and grew, it seemed I could not finish it. It took time to understand why I ought not to write it at all.

It first struck me after a three-day large group workshop; I had been both organizer and participant, had been attacked on the first day, received symbolic bouquets later. I had tried to be an ordinary member nonetheless. And, when I recovered from the fatigue, I reflected on the group process. The conductor, a guest from abroad, had said to me in the car: 'I studied with Foulkes, but everyone has to learn for themselves how to take a group.'

Plausible. And does the same group experience mean different things to different people? In the following year's workshop, a larger group than before, I tried to summarize, in my mind, the very rich content of the group. A colleague had driven the conductor back to his residence on this occasion. 'They wanted to kill the father on the first day, and then repented,' was how he summarized it to her. He had twice made a mistake about the timing of breaks and interrupted some interesting developments. Hence he was attacked. But was this the essence of the group process?

It would seem that the content of a meeting or sequence of meetings of a group-analytic group is rich and near-incommunicable. Sandison (1998, p.65) writes: 'After a group it is not necessarily what anyone says that remains in the memory; it is the feeling-tone which the session engendered.' He holds that 'the experience of being and belonging to a group need not involve the use of linear memory at all.' Further, 'the source of cohesion comes from the growth of the feeling tone memory which has its origin in unconscious and ancestral processes akin to what happened when we listened to stories in our earliest years, usually while in close contact with a parent' (Sandison 1998, p.63).

Sandison mentions the Dymock poets who formed a group in Gloucestershire between 1911 and 1915, the memory of the experience being rendered in poetry.

> Do you remember that still summer evening
> When in the cosy cream-washed living-room
> Of the Old Nail shop, we all talked and laughed...

To put it another way, though we can describe characteristics of the group process logically and scientifically, an important component is ineluctable and unfathomable, unique to each group and to each group analyst with each particular group.

I do not believe that psychotherapy is about the triumph of the rational, of secondary process, over the intuitive, primary process. Rycroft (1979, p.158) stressed the importance of primary process, especially in creativity. He held that primary and secondary process coexist from the start, and 'continue to function in harmony with one another, one providing the imaginative, the other the rational basis of living.' Rather than abolish the unconscious, we need to improve our relationship with it. Using Freud's metaphor, we learn to swim in the Zuider Sea rather than dry it up.

Learning to practise group psychotherapy is not a guided tour through the body of knowledge on the subject. Training institutes acknowledge this fact by requiring candidates to undergo a personal group experience, just as psychoanalytic training requires a personal analysis (though this may have other aspects). One cannot, as in chemical analysis, learn the practice through step-by-step instruction.

There are many ways of conducting a group-analytic group. Dalal (1995, pp.379–393) points to the different possibilities with which the group conductor is constantly faced: 'any interaction will be a communication of certain things and simultaneously an avoidance of communicating certain other things.' He asks which is more therapeutic, to think or to feel. The old psychoanalytic model argues that repeated expression in action of a trauma results in remaining blind to it. Conversely, the Cathartic model – originally Freud-Breuer, then Reich and followers – works towards release of blocked emotions, locked away in muscular tensions. Dalal argues that both thought and feeling are essential for change to occur.

Dalal reminds us of the elevation of thought over feeling in Western philosophy as well as in psychoanalysis. It occurs to me that this is true of philosophers from Plato onwards, until Sartre pioneered a theory of emotion.

Let us look at psychoanalysis, where Matte Blanco (1975, p.221) developed a theory, dividing emotion into sensation-feeling and thinking components. His main example of sensation-feeling is pain – which is not an emotion. He suggests that unconscious sensations may be the basis of some feelings.

In the thinking component, he notes generalization, maximization and irradiation. Generalization is 'confusion of the individual with the class' (Matte Blanco 1975, p.245). Why confusion? Do we 'confuse' the feared object with the class of all feared objects, or do we correctly classify as a dangerous object? The function of fear is protective, and the emotion is often instant and intuitive, working faster than rational reflection could. We are not, after all, discussing phobia.

I say this not to detract from Matte Blanco's brilliant analysis, but to illustrate the difficulty of discussing and describing emotion in cognitive language and of getting away from the body-mind model.

Matte Blanco (1975) discusses 'the translating function' and illustrates with a clinical example: a patient's reaction to an announcement that he would take ten days off to complete some writing. He describes the complex process of arriving at an interpretation: the patient felt the same unbearable feelings about the analyst's symbolic pregnancy that he had done when his mother gave birth to and suckled his baby sister. While it is true that the analyst reached this conclusion through a thinking process, it surely would have meant nothing to the patient, and been ineffective, had it not carried a high emotional charge – as the author himself might well agree.

The elevation of thinking reaches its peak in the linguistic philosophy of our day, which asserts everything can be stated in language, and with the perfection of linguistic statement all philosophical problems will disappear. But, as Magee (1997) points out, language cannot even do justice to the richness of what he sees before him in his study. Let us consider music: many of us can differentiate between the style of Beethoven, Brahms and Britten. Two bars may suffice for me to think 'Sibelius'. Yet the characteristics of each cannot be adequately expressed in cognitive language. Our ability to recognize faces defies language and it is difficult to program a computer to do this (Copeland and Proudfoot 1999, p.99.)

Consider emotion again; most of us know what 'remorse' is. We could describe some of its characteristics: regret, guilt feelings, a desire to make amends, a resolve to change. Yet our knowledge of whether we genuinely feel it transcends any verbal definition.

The group process is like a tree. It could, at any moment, branch off in different directions. The therapist has to be aware of the multiple meanings of what happens at any point in time. There is no one right way to intervene, or refrain from doing so. There is scope for the therapist's sensitivity and creativity, so long as it does not inhibit the creativity of the group.

PART 2

Special Kinds of Groups

CHAPTER 9

Groups with Psychotic and Borderline Personalities

Group-analytic principles, the use of the group as therapist, can very well be applied to patients who are actively psychotic, have been psychotic or have borderline personalities: all the kinds of patients usually believed to be unsuitable or difficult subjects for psychotherapy. Foulkes himself held that the occasional psychotic member might be included in a group. This has been done in the Group Analytic Practice, London and described by Kreeger (1991). Foulkes himself did not run a group all of whose members were psychotic, nor had much been written about such groups by his followers until the appearance of *Group Psychotherapy of the Psychoses* (Schermer and Pines 1999). Until then, Kanas was usually cited as the only authority for work with psychotics. His method is structured rather than group analytic; he holds the group to discussion of specific themes. Among group-analytic approaches, Urlic (1999, p.155) emphasizes that the group itself is the main therapeutic factor, and the importance of 'the attenuation and dissolution of the transference to the therapist'. Schneider (1999, pp.194–196) shows how the therapist's empathy guides the choice of the interpretation which will not be damaging. Resnick (1999, p.124), after forty years of listening to psychotics, writes: 'patients are able to gain much understanding as long as the analyst refrains from intruding too much in the language of a particular psychoanalytic school, above all, he has to listen and learn sharing with them unexpected intuitive discoveries which lead to interpretations.'

In my own work in the public sector, I have developed, over some forty years, a model for such groups (probably not the only one, as others seem to have done similar work).

The model applies to inpatient and outpatient work, though each setting has its specific problems. As my outpatient groups constitute my more recent (and current) experience, with a slow-open group twenty years old at the time of writing, most of my illustrations will be taken from this setting.

How can the group of psychotics be therapist?

One may well ask how a group of persons as sick as acute or chronic schizo-phrenics can be therapist. A simple answer is that they, like all human beings, have a need to be needed, and experience shows that they can rise to the occasion.

The development of their abilities depends to some extent on the therapist's expectations and on mutual trust. Just as a child's individuation and growth towards autonomy depends on the parents' ability to trust and let him grow, so it is with the group.

Foulkes (1948, p.31) deals with the question of neurotics healing one another. He holds that though the individual group member may be neurotic, the group norm is towards health: what the group supports, 'quite blindly and instinctively, is determined…by its survival value.' He perceives the neurotic symptom as an expression of interpersonal problems. The group cannot understand symptom language, but when translated into interpersonal language the problems are intel-ligible to all and can be discussed in the group.

We find that psychotic symptoms, too, can be translated into interpersonal language, making it possible for the group to deal with them. The group of psychotics seems to have a group norm that is healthy. The group tends to criticize members who take no interest in others, who do not help themselves, who make excessive demands on their family or, conversely, do not stand up for themselves. This begins with perceiving the needs of the group and is extended to the world outside.

The temptation to be the only therapist
(or to abandon group analysis)

Once, when I was a junior on a psychiatric observation unit in England, the consultant in charge said to me: 'After all, I am the only therapist here.' The context is forgotten, but the remark remains in my memory. Technically, it may have been true, he was the only qualified one; yet it was a slap in the face. I reflected that I worked ten hours a day and worked well. The remark implied opacity, superiority, inaccessibility. It is a remark that a group analyst should never make, explicitly or implicitly.

Foulkes emphasized that the group itself is the instrument of therapy, not merely a background. The therapist's task is to forge and perfect this instrument, not to be the only therapist. A conductor training a choir could not sing all the parts alone.

In the group of psychotics, at least two factors tempt the conductor to be soloist (or at least a central figure): the great dependency needs of the patients, and the medical model.

Dependency needs

The factor that most members of psychotics groups have in common, characteristically, is immature personality. (The patient who suffers from bipolar disorder but is mature will probably have found his way into a group of neurotics.)

One manic-depressive woman in my group, a mother of two children, at first appeared to observers to be relatively healthy. They soon realized that she had an irresistible need to be the centre of attention, both in the group and at home, like a very young child. Such patients seem to cry out for special attention, for answers, for the solutions to burning problems that the therapist can give so well.

The therapist easily becomes convinced that it is up to him or her to make individual interpretations, which may be a case of complementary counter-transference (Racker 1968). If the therapist gives in to it, other group members will demand similar attention. Instead of the previous sharing, there will be competition for parental attention – and for parental time; there is never enough. The belief that one can never give enough will become a self-fulfilling prophecy. One co-therapist, who could be good at responding appropriately to individuals, said after one such group: 'There is not enough to go round. The blanket is too short.' This, indeed, is the position when therapists act on the belief that they alone can treat the group. Their own well-meant efforts, however, are destructive of the group process, destructive of members' autonomy. The therapist can easily be tempted to be an overprotective mother to the group.

What is required of the therapist is to be a good-enough mother – no more and no less.

Medical model

The medical model is one to which many of the patients are accustomed, as well as some therapists. The doctor is authoritarian or benignly paternalistic; the patient is subservient. The 'good patient' is 'compliant'. It is clear that this model is not conducive to autonomy of group members, or of the group as a whole.

Structure and didacticism

Making groups structured and didactic is another temptation. I find myself occasionally tempted to be didactic, but I hope that I do this in the Socratic way, encouraging the group to find its own answer. Kanas (1993) holds that groups for psychotics should be structured; for schizophrenics' groups he prescribes the discussion of specific topics 'related to hearing voices, feeling suspicious, being confused, and relating poorly with other people'. This is no doubt helpful and efficient, but it prevents the evolution of the spontaneous group process. Yalom (1981) holds that inpatient groups do best when structured, both to prevent raising levels of anxiety and because time is short: in acute wards turnover is rapid and there should be a single-session time frame. I have found, however, that unstructured groups work excellently in admission units.

Turning the group into an instrument of therapy

Certainly, the conductor has to be more active in groups with psychotics: not, however, in leading or in 'direct therapy', but in training the group and turning it into an instrument of therapy. Here, briefly, are some means of doing this.

Translation of symptoms

An important issue is the translation of symptoms into interpersonal problems. Foulkes (1948) has written about neurotic symptoms being expressions of inter-personal difficulties. This holds good for psychotic symptoms and is a key factor in the communication network of the group.

Foulkes (1948, p.30) writes: 'Now, neurotic peculiarities, symptoms, are relieved just as much, as they can be retransformed, by Analysis, from unshareable to shareable experience, from incommunicable to communicable experience.' The symptom is an expression of an interpersonal problem.

The group, indeed, cannot understand symptoms, referring them to the group conductor, especially if he or she is a doctor.

Group members with immature personalities are more likely than others to use symptom language. Ruesch and Bateson (1951) point out that the immature patient may communicate by the means used in early childhood, transmitting messages involving pain or touch, conveyed by short-distance receivers, rather than sight or hearing which operate at longer distances. These patients assume that others use the same system of psychosomatic codification and, thus, that they are part of the same physical matrix. Incidentally, the same holds good for patients with psychosomatic disorders, who deny any intrapsychic or interpersonal problems.

Whether group members complain of a somatic symptom, or hide behind a diagnostic label, like feeling 'depressed', the task is to ask what is happening in their lives, what goes on between themselves and others. The group soon learns to ask these questions, encouraging the protagonist to translate symptoms into inter-personal problems. Thus, Shira complains that she is depressed, she cannot cope. The group asks what has been happening. Has she quarrelled with her partner? Is there a problem with one of her children? Sometimes the translation reveals new vistas.

Ex. 9(i). Eric, a bachelor of 45, opened the meeting with a question: should he go on a ramble with his friends despite having an earache? The group asked why he was talking about earache. He replied that what really bothered him was that his father did not want him to go. To this, group members could relate. Shira said she certainly would not ask her father's permission if she were in Eric's place. Eric was, after all, grown up. Others joined in. For the first time, Eric discussed some of the problems arising out of his symbiotic relationship with his father.

The group-centred orientation

Figures 9.1 and 9.2 illustrate a leader-centred group and group-centred group respectively.

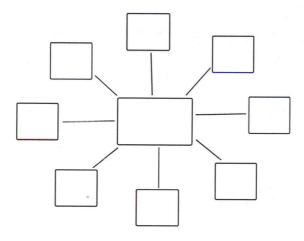

Figure 9.1 Leader-centred group (adapted from Folkes)

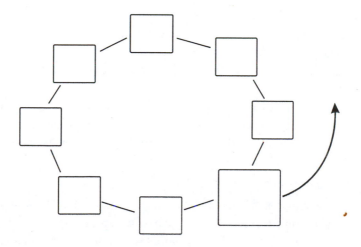

Figure 9.2 Group-centred group (adapted from Folkes)

The therapist of the psychotic group has to keep Figure 9.2 in mind, and start off on the right foot. As already mentioned, it is easy to view group members' demands for individual attention as needs. The conductor, particularly if he is a doctor, may perceive himself as a benign paternal authority who has all the answers. The result will be a leader-centred group (Figure 9.1).

It is not the case that schizophrenics are unable to relate to one another in groups. Research by Salzberg (1962, cited in Bloch and Crouch 1985) examined four modes of therapist behaviour:

1. silence (contributing only when necessary)

2. talking (contributing when conversation lags)

3. redirecting (involving another patient if a patient speaks to the therapist)

4. directing (addressing the patient who has spoken without reference to the others).

One experimental group used active talking and directing, the second silence and redirecting. It was found that talking and directing led to less interaction, silence and redirecting to more interaction. This study was carried out with acute psychotic inpatients.

It is important for the therapist to resist the temptation to make individual interpretations. Every individual response increases the expectation for more such responses, decreasing responses by the group. Instead, the therapist should redirect, make sure group members' observations are heard, expand on them and sharpen focus.

Redirecting

When a group member addresses the therapist, she asks this group member to address the group. At the same time, or alternatively, the group is asked to respond. A gesture may be enough to indicate both. The group soon learns that it is expected to respond, as does the erring member, but there may be regression at times of stress.

It often happens that a group member reverts to symptom language or discusses drug therapy. Since the member knows that the group cannot speak this language, I tend to interpret this as a demand for individual attention.

Making sure communications are heard

Some group members speak in a way that ensures they will not be heard, either by wrong timing or indistinctness. One woman would speak quickly and indistinctly, as if the years had taught her that her words were not listened to and not worth listening to. One might ask the group if they had understood; in time the group learnt to ask her to speak more slowly.

Confirming

One member may make a particularly apt observation. Schizophrenics are often very sensitive to the unconscious of others and may hit the nail on the head. To avoid this observation being lost in a sea of indifferent ones, it is as well to draw attention to it.

> Ex. 9(ii). Pat, a new member, was asked why she had joined. 'The doctor was after me until I did...actually, I have a problem with the time.' Betty replied that everyone had; she had been rushing off from work to get here. The therapist pointed out that this is not what Pat had in mind; she had a problem with the children.

> Pat burst into tears. 'I think I'm doing to my children exactly what my parents did to me.' She described how she was abandoned as a child. The group tried to comfort her in various ways. Iris said something different: 'It is not a good thing to go to the other extreme, to spoil them. That's not psychologically sound.' The group appeared to ignore this, and someone advised Pat to forget the past. I pointed out that Iris had said something important.

Therapeutic factors specific to the group with psychotic patients

Under this heading I shall discuss:

- learning to communicate (the two components)
- finding 'friends in suffering'
- perception of self and others
- being accepted as an equal and being given responsibility
- being able to make a difference to the other.

Learning to communicate (the two components)

We have already discussed one component of communication: the matter of common language. There are many kinds of private language; symptom language is only one of them. Patients may indicate their feelings by the tone they use. They may talk in a whining tone, like an infant expecting sympathy and succour as a response to their crying. In individual therapy, the therapist often plays the role of mother to an inarticulate baby, often guessing and interpreting, rather than encouraging the patient to be more articulate. In the group, the patient himself has to translate communications into common language; the group is therefore less encouraging of dependence than individual therapy.

The other component of communication is creating, and engaging in, the web of group dialogue. As de Maré put it (personal communication), one has to learn to talk in the group. The group member has to have the courage to take up space, but not too much space; not to monopolize, or to engage in an exclusive dialogue with one other, but to let the ball go round. We might call this the syntax of group communication, as opposed to the language.

Immature personalities have great problems with the syntax. At the most basic level, they are like small children who burst in to address the parents, disregarding the subject of conversation. The next stage is to do this politely, wait for a natural break, preface one's words with the equivalent of 'excuse me', as small children are taught to do.

But the communication is still isolated, out of context. A further stage is 'turn-taking'. One member waits till the other has finished, but is so intent on her own thing that she has not been able to relate to the other, at least not more than formally.

I do not formally teach group members the syntax of communication. They learn that the group dialogue is the best thing there is, better than engaging the therapist. In fact, if the therapist refuses to be engaged, they learn that group dialogue is all there is. The group itself learns to promote the group dialogue: it notices when members have failed to relate to the remarks of one of them, and rebukes them for cutting others short.

Finding 'friends in suffering'

Yalom (1981) described a therapeutic factor he called 'universality': many a patient believes he is unique in having unacceptable impulses or fantasies; in the group he finds he is not alone after all, as others have similar problems. The patient who is or has been psychotic, in his isolation, is even more likely than the neurotic to believe that his problem is unique, and suffer a good deal of anxiety on this account. It takes courage to take the plunge and reveal the problem to the group. Some do not venture until another group member has done so. To hear that another suffers from a problem similar to one's own brings great relief.

> Ex. 9(iii). Dan believed that his thoughts had been put into his head by means of an EEG machine. He had been very reluctant to reveal this. When he did, Yochanan confided that he too had suffered from this kind of thing. Yochanan had never talked of this before. He had, with some difficulty, revealed that 'the doctors' had been arranging girls for him; he had expressed doubts if the group would understand; only a doctor would. Now he was glad to hear he was not the only one who had 'thoughts put into his head'; both group members benefited.

> Interestingly, Yochanan's problems diminished in the course of time. He later complained about problems in the radio and in the television set. The group offered advice on the practical and other levels. The obvious interpretation was

difficulty in communication, though making this observation had little effect. One may surmise that it was too threatening for him to consider his basic difficulty in communicating with others.

Perception of self and others

In previous writings, (Chazan 1993b), I talked about 'reality testing', but this has, I think, authoritarian connotations: that we all share a common reality; that the psychotic is out of step; we must make him or her conform. Perhaps the practice in totalitarian countries of treating dissenters in mental hospitals has further sharpened this connotation.

I am not concerned if a patient has strange associations to colours, so long as he knows that a red traffic-light means 'stop'. What matters is our ability to know what is expected of us, to be sensitive to the signals given to us by others, to know how to behave in a specific context. It is our perception of self and others that is important, our ability to see them as they see themselves, to perceive ourselves as we are perceived by them. This involves being flexible in perceiving oneself and others (see Chapter 6).

Autistic persons, even highly intelligent ones, are deficient in these abilities. They have to learn painstakingly what comes naturally to most of us, which is why Oliver Sacks' (1995) science graduate spoke of herself as being 'like an anthropologist from Mars'.

To remind us how we acquire these abilities, let us return to Bateson's (1972[1935]) theory of levels of learning (see Chapter 6). Learning One concerns the adaptive response. Learning Two is the identification of context, as different contexts require different responses. Learning Two is personal and subjective; it is acquired early in infancy and mostly unconsciously. Bateson speaks of character traits as part of Learning Two: character is relationship, a mode of relating to others.

Learning Two can be adaptive or non-adaptive. One model of neurosis is non-adaptive L2. Learning Two is self-validating; no fact in reality can ever disprove it. Moreover, the person who believes that people hate him will behave in a way that brings this about. Being self-validating, L2 is almost ineradicable.

In psychotherapy, the patient relates to the therapist as if the therapist were a person from the patient's past. This relating is termed transference.

Learning Three is the transformation of Learning Two. It can be brought about by psychotherapy, not without difficulty. It entails not merely replacement of maladaptive reactions by adaptive ones, but the facilitation of such replacement.

Experience with paranoid schizophrenics confirms the self-validating nature of Learning Two: no factual evidence ever convinces them that their view is distorted, or induces them to modify it. I would suggest that what characterizes the paranoid psychotic is not so much the wrongness of the perception as the rigidity with which it is held.

The group is an excellent medium for altering Learning Two, because of the multiplicity of perceptions available. Confrontation with one single alternative reality is not as effective. Instead of black–white, right–wrong, digital confrontation, we have the analogic colour palette of the group.

Being accepted as an equal and being given responsibility

In the acute phase of illness, it is appropriate to put a moratorium on responsibility, to ask the patient to make no important decisions and allow himself to be protected. However, this state of affairs is often prolonged. In hospital settings, we often hear the phrase: 'Let him be responsible for himself, responsibility for others can come later.' Yet it is part of life to be responsible for others: our children, other members of our family, as well as specific tasks in our working lives. To be deprived of responsibility for others is a severe narcissistic injury.

In therapeutic communities, sharing responsibility with patients has been found to be a potent therapeutic factor (see Chapter 11).

As to being treated as an equal, this is often sadly lacking in the experience of the post-psychotic patient in the community. Even in accepting and affectionate families, this is not so; the post-psychotic is frequently treated as a perpetual child who has to be protected.

In our groups, the group member is given to understand that she shares responsibility with the therapist; she is expected to listen to others, relate to what they say, understand, be supportive or critical, advise or interpret. She learns that, outside the group, she is responsible for her own life and for her relationships with significant others.

Being able to make a difference to the other

Laing (1961, pp.66–72) writes of the importance of complementarity. A mother cannot be a mother without a child. A child needs not only to receive from his mother, but also needs to be allowed to give. 'The good breast is a breast that can receive as well as give.'

Emptiness not only is physical, but also can be experienced when there is lack of meaning in life. 'Emptiness and futility can arise when a person has put himself into his acts, even when these acts seem to have some point to him, if he is accorded no recognition by the other, and if he feels he is not able to make any difference to anyone' (Laing 1961, p.67).

On first coming to the group, the psychotic is surprised that he is expected to help others. Is he not sick himself? The conductor makes it clear that this is exactly what **is** expected. In time, the psychotic or post-psychotic group member discovers in himself the ability to listen and understand, to show sympathy or be critical, to comment and advise. He is needed and valuable in the group.

We find that group members can make valid clarifications and interpretations.

> Ex. 9(iv). Daniel was married after some two years in the group. We had asked his wife, Deborah, to join the group as well. A daughter was born to them – the baby of the group. Aviva, the daughter, was 5 when the following dialogue occurred. Deborah brought a problem: when Daniel came home from work, Aviva wanted to play with him. He, on the other hand, was tired and wanted to rest. On one occasion the little one had woken her father; he reacted automatically by giving her a slap. What should one do? It was wrong to slap her; but she had also to learn to respect her father. The group discussed this for a while, then Aaron came up with an idea. He suggested that Daniel, on coming home, rest with a cup of coffee for about ten minutes, and then play with Aviva for about half an hour. The couple accepted this idea.

> Considering that Aaron was childless, and had never been able to cope with the noise of small nephews and nieces, this was an excellent piece of lateral thinking on his part.

The group of psychotics as therapist

Foulkes (1948, p.121) shows that the group can make interpretations. This is true of the group of psychotic patients.

> Ex. 9(v). In one meeting, Deborah had once more brought a problem concerning her little girl. 'You know,' said Bernie, 'you always talk about Aviva's problems, never about the problems between Daniel and yourself.' Now Deborah brought what was apparently a marital problem: the two of them were planning to go out to dinner one evening, and Daniel had told his parents. Deborah did not think that parents ought to know what went on between husband and wife. This was a rule of theirs. The group discussed the matter of a couple keeping things to themselves.

> I remarked that Deborah was also telling the group that problems between husband and wife were confidential and not for the ears of the group. On the other hand, we had been wondering why she was taking all the childcare upon herself, rather than involving Daniel, who was willing and able to play the paternal role.

> She ignored the interpretation, but took up the matter of involving her husband. Daniel was taking stronger drugs than she, she argued. Daniel told the group that he did play with Aviva each day, and made her sandwich each morning.

> Bernie's interpretation was correct and very much to the point. Deborah almost always discussed problems of mothering in the group. She saw herself as the principal parent, leaving very little space for Daniel. She indeed called the shots

and made the rules in the family. She was reluctant to bring the marital relationship into the group and Daniel was afraid to do so.

Reflecting on this several months later, we found that Deborah was bringing marital issues not infrequently.

Thus, the group is able to give sound advice (which may not be appropriate for the therapist). It can also make interpretations, which, as we know, are more acceptable coming from them than from the therapist. Conversely, the group member who can be effective in this way is strengthened by his ability to make a difference to others.

Unconscious understanding

Foulkes (1948, p.120) describes unconscious understanding by the group. As one might expect, the unconscious of the psychotics group is a fertile field in every respect. It is worth the therapist's while to look for unconscious connections between subjects brought up in the group: by the law of free-floating discussion, the equivalent of free association, there are likely to be such connections even when issues seem disparate. More than that, what may appear like a schizophrenic non sequitur could be meaningful.

> Ex. 9(vi). In one meeting, members were complaining of going unheard by others; each brought a problem which seemed to fall on deaf ears. Peter interjected a Talmudic tale: 'One day Kamza was riding on a horse, when a poor man asked for food. He said he was hungry himself and would not get off his horse until he had eaten. As a punishment, his hands withered.'
>
> 'What does this have to do with what we are talking about?' a group member asked angrily. 'He does not relate to what we're saying at all,' said Avram. 'He does not relate to his own son; what do you expect?' said Deborah.
>
> 'Perhaps his story is relevant after all,' I said. 'Everyone in the group is so hungry and needy that he cannot spare a thought for others.'

The use of metaphor by the therapist

The group finds metaphor used by the therapist acceptable and meaningful.

> Ex. 9(vii). The meeting was shortly before the Jewish New Year, which is associated with repentance and reviewing of one's actions.
>
> Aaron said he wanted to wish his neighbour a happy New Year, but feared that he might be rejected. Helen expressed doubts about whether people liked her. Peter had been wondering how he would be received at his nephew's bar mitzvah celebration; in fact, it went off all right.

There was much talk about help from Heaven, even about the Messiah. Daniel, who was the most religious group member, countered this by stressing the need to help oneself. There were isolated appeals for help and little comment on one another's problems.

I told the story from S.Y. Agnon's 'Days of Awe' I have described in Chapter 7, p.83. I added that the group today seemed like the man lost in the forest. 'Yes,' said Simon, 'maybe the group is like a wood'.

Existential aspects of the group

When the group has learnt to translate symptom language into the language of interpersonal relationships and of emotions, the group dialogue centres mostly around interpersonal problems and, beyond that, the existential problems common to all of us; freedom or the lack of it, being respected by others versus being thought 'different', being loved and being lovable, living with others, roles in family life and role conflicts, and, above all, loneliness.

These existential issues arise most commonly in long-term patients living in the community, who have time to think about the nature of their lives. In acute hospital wards much is happening in a short space of time, and chronic wards are often so structured as to prevent anything from happening.

Freedom versus determinism

Freedom to determine our lives is of course an issue for all of us, but is more often questioned by patients who have been psychotic. They talk about 'the illness', believing that only fate or a miracle can change their lives. They talk about 'the illness' ruling their lives, about being unable to help doing what they do. Although there may be areas of their lives they may not be able to control, it is important for them to take responsibility for all they can. (With acute patients, we may want to put a moratorium on responsibility.)

> Ex. 9(viii). Shira suffers from bipolar disorder. She is divorced, lives with a long-term partner, and has a married daughter with a young son. She was telling the group that her daughter complained that she visited too often, and did not let her know in advance. The group told her that she ought to let her daughter know. 'I can do what I like,' she replied. ' I am manic and cannot help what I do.' We helped her to understand that she was exploiting her illness and pleading lack of responsibility. This sort of behaviour would not pay off and it would be better if she behaved responsibly.

Controlling anger

A frequent issue is controlling anger, as against being controlled by it. The members of our group often have good cause to be angry.

Ex. 9(ix). Aaron, a divorced man who lives alone, was cut dead by all his brothers and sisters since his mother died. They even had her sign a will, on her deathbed, stating that he was to be disinherited on the grounds of being a hospitalized patient (which he was not). He was always angry at what fate had done to him, now he was more so. He would talk about setting his siblings' houses on fire. The group got him to see that this would be wrong. When a lawyer discovered that the will would not be valid unless he agreed, he refused to sign. 'They will have nothing, and I will have nothing.' I thought that this would be a legitimate way of expressing his anger and did not dissuade him. (I pointed out, however, that his signature alone would not get him a share, as the family told him, but he would have to consult a lawyer of his own.)

At one time, Aaron used to act violently when angry. He had once, when he mother was still alive, trodden on a bottle in a family row. He broke the bottle and splintered the small bones of his foot. His sister came to demand hospitalization. My co-therapist and I decided to have him sign a declaration that he would not be violent against himself or against others. This worked. Often, he would report instances of self-control of which he was proud. A man had provoked him on the bus; he felt like hitting him, but did nothing. When Peter lost his temper in the group or reported instances of angry outbursts, Aaron was able to point to the value of self-control.

Being respected and esteemed versus considered 'different'

We all have a need to be esteemed and respected by others. Post-psychotic patients may doubt whether they are respected in the community. (This is both the result of low self-esteem and a reflection of reality, since the mentally ill are stigmatized.) Deborah would express such doubts about herself and her daughter who was in kindergarten. She had sent a New Year card to the kindergarten teacher. Was that all right? Did the mothers consider her 'different', or like one of them? Did they perceive her daughter as 'different' or just like other children?

Needing to be loved

The need to be loved is universal. Schizophrenics often entertain doubts as to whether they are lovable, even if they feel loved by their parents.

Ex. 9(x). Helen was in her late thirties when she joined the group. Schizophrenic since the age of 17, she had difficulties in social contact. When she first came to the group, she dressed unattractively. Gradually, she began to care about her appearance. 'Today you look sexy,' a male group member would say. From doing nothing, living at home with her parents, she progressed to staying with her sister in Ramat Gan and helping with her children. She continued to come to Jerusalem for the group. She began to work in a sheltered workshop.

As her parents were ageing, they thought about arranging a marriage for Helen. There was one disastrous affair, when Helen was persuaded to cohabit with her prospective partner, though this was against all her instincts and against her religious principles. Some time later, she was introduced to a librarian who was a philosophy graduate. (I happened to know him and knew he was brilliant; I did not tell her of my acquaintance to avoid embarrassing her.) Being an albino and visibly short-sighted, he may have found it difficult to find a partner. Helen married him, was very happy and felt she was loved by her husband. She repeatedly reflected several times in the group that she was very fortunate and could not believe her luck.

'How could anyone love me? Am I really lovable?'

There are those who have a constant need to test the love of members of their family.

> Ex. 9(xi). Shira complains that her son does not really love her, otherwise he would not go off on a holiday in the Far East for three months (at the age of 21). He has a girlfriend and she is jealous. When her children were younger, she would complain that they did not visit often. They ought to have more consideration for a sick mother. From Shira's behaviour in the group, one could infer that at home too she complained and whined a lot about how she felt. This was probably an unconscious attempt to engage her children's sympathies, but had the opposite effect. We reflected this to her.

Roles and role conflicts

Those in the group who are married have to work out their role as spouses: how to live with a partner, and yet be oneself. How much does one expect of the other and do for the other? How does one find ways of living one's own life and leave the other free?

> Ex. 9(xii). Shira complains bitterly that her long-term partner studies for long hours after work instead of devoting time to her. The group asks if she is not proud of him. It has not occurred to her. Why does she not go to the social club? Her partner does not want her to mix with other sick people. We know her well enough to understand that she uses this as an excuse; she will not make the effort to get involved in the club. Besides, if she went out more she would no longer have a grievance.

> Ex. 9(xiii). Deborah often talks about her mother and her sisters, and their influence on her. The group points out that she is a married woman; what she does is a matter of agreement between her husband and herself. Daniel, her husband, recalls that during the Gulf War there was a song about 'going home'. He asked a Rabbi which was home – his father's house or his married home? The answer was that the couples' house was home.

Ex. 9(xiv). Since her marriage, Helen frequently says she spends a lot of time with her parents, goes to visit them several times a day. They are old and sick; she wants to help them, to honour them. Although at first this looks like a role conflict, it becomes clear that Helen has a pathological need to be with her parents. She finds it hard to be separated from them. Sometimes she talks about 'making sure they are all right', at others expresses fears they might die if she left them. She appears to have ideas of magical powers. It seems, also, that the symbiotic link with her parents is still powerful.

Loneliness

The pain of loneliness is universal. People who have been psychotic are more likely to be exposed to it than the rest of us: characteristically, they have no friends.

Ex. 9(xv). Aaron makes it clear that he cannot be with people. Even the social work student who visits him becomes a burden after a few minutes. When his mother was still alive, he could not bear the presence of his young nephews and nieces. He was thus between the devil and the deep sea: to be with others was unbearable, to be alone was bleak.

Ex. 9(xvi). Bernie has been divorced for several years; he has six grown-up children. Two years ago his brother was killed in a suicide bombing. It turned out that he was the sibling with whom he had the closest relationship. Since then, Bernie often complains of loneliness. Yes, he goes to the social club. He is successful there; he has been elected to the committee. When President Weizman's wife visited the club, he was chosen to read the welcoming speech. However, once at home he feels he is alone. Bernie recently complained of fear of something unknown. It is not easy to get him to define what it is all about. Recently he was able to do so. 'I sometimes think that if I die no one will know, I will just rot.' The group enquire into relations with his family. It turns out that there is no one with whom he is in touch, no one who enquires about his welfare. He is offended easily. He was offended by something his sister said, perhaps rightly; yet when the sister made gestures of reconciliation, he rejected them. He complained that she should have done so earlier. He often hints that he believes his family regard him as a burden; evidently, his self-esteem is extremely low. Thus he remains with his loneliness.

Post-psychotic patients may learn to live alone, though it is difficult for them to learn to live with their loneliness. What is even more difficult is for them to learn to be sufficient unto themselves and to value themselves. It is only then that they can learn to relate to others.

CHAPTER 10

The Multiple Family Therapy Group

The multiple family therapy group is a compound group, a group made up of groups. It is a group-analytic group composed of natural groups. The group process is made use of to influence the dynamics of the component family groups.

A multiple family group can be made up of all kinds of families. One possibility is the group of families of psychotic patients, which will be the subject of this chapter. Foulkes considered family therapy important; he regarded family group therapy and group-analytic therapy as related. Foulkes (1975, p.13) writes that he would see family members (although analysts usually refrain from doing so). He saw work with the family as particularly important in the case of psychotics, especially schizophrenics, where 'the interrelation with the family, both in a horizontal and vertical way is particularly easy to see.' He mentions the work of T. Lidz, R.D. Scott, R.D. Laing and A. Esterson.

I had the good fortune to work for R.D. Scott at Napsbury, near St. Albans, Hertfordshire, for several years, and to attend seminars by R.D. Laing. In Jerusalem, I conducted a multiple family therapy group on an admission unit for psychotic adults for eight years. This potentiated the treatment of many patients, and in some cases seemed to be the critical component that made all the difference.

There is no reason why a similar group should not be run for the families of post-psychotic patients in an outpatient clinic. It may, however, be more difficult to find families willing to commit themselves. A crisis such as admission usually spurs families to seek help and hence they can be recruited to the group. Families of outpatients do occasionally call for help with their difficulties; if the identified patient agrees, and if there are at least four such families, a group can be formed.

Theoretical assumptions

Working with such a multiple family therapy group presupposes four theoretical assumptions.

The adult personality is vulnerable to the present influence of the family

According to psychoanalytic theory, the foundations of personality are laid in infancy, under the influence of parents and other significant adults. Psychoanalysis treats the individual and his introjects of significant others. It bases itself on linear, vertical causality; events in the individual's past are assumed to have made him what he is. The systems theory of family therapy points to another kind of causality which is circular: modes of relating in the present have a reciprocal influence. One can point to no original cause, nor has any one family member 'caused' pathology in another; influences are mutual. Laing and Esterson (1964) have studied patients diagnosed as schizophrenic together with their families. They consider the concept of 'family pathology' to be a confused one and replace it by 'unintelligibility'. Following Sartre, they distinguish between 'process', which is interaction in a group not intended by anyone, and 'praxis', intended action. According to this model, parents are not labelled 'schizophrenogenic' and no guilt is attributed.

The anthropologist Gregory Bateson, with Jackson, Haley and Weakland, pioneered research on schizophrenics and their families. Bateson *et al.* (1956) pointed to the inability of schizophrenics to distinguish between communicational modes, both in messages received, messages uttered by them and their own thinking. They may use metaphors without labelling them as such. The authors describe the 'Double Bind' situation created by significant family members: a primary negative injunction, a conflicting secondary injunction, and a third injunction prohibiting escape from the field. This leads to an untenable position; schizophrenia is the outcome of such a situation.

Disturbance in the family process does not imply guilt on anyone's part

This follows from what has been said in the preceding assumption. It should be borne in mind and, if necessary, explained to family members, as dynamic and systemic family therapy is widely believed to attribute blame to the family. The more recent 'psycho-educative approach' claims its 'no-blame' theory to be an advantage. Christopher Dare, in a conference workshop held in London in 1992, reported on using the best of both worlds: he attracted families with the psycho-educative approach and then explained to them that schizophrenics were particularly sensitive and vulnerable, therefore requiring special modes of relating on the family's part.

The family can sabotage attempts to treat the designated patient

Since the family strives for homoeostasis, it is not surprising that change in the designated patient is resisted. Hence, it is important to include the family in the patient's treatment in an effective way.

The group-analytic model can be adapted to family therapy

I assumed that, just as group-analytic therapy is effective for the individual group member, family group therapy is effective for the equivalent component of the group, namely, the family. That it indeed works can be shown to be true only by experience (and, indeed, the group proved itself over a period of eight years).

Previous work with multiple family therapy groups has been described by Laqueur, Le Bart and Morong (1964), Hes and Handler (1961), Curry (1965), Barcai (1967), Leichter and Shulman (1966), while Levin (1966) as well as Davies, Ellenson and Young (1966) specifically described the open type of family group.

I ran a multiple family therapy group on an acute admission ward for eight years. It was a slow-open group, run on group-analytic principles. Let us see how it worked.

Background

A multiple family therapy group was begun in July 1968 on the admission unit of Kfar Shaul Hospital, Jerusalem, a mixed 32-bedded unit which was then receiving admissions from Jerusalem and the southern part of Israel, at the rate of between eight and twelve weekly. Group therapy was central to the treatment of the patients. There were thrice weekly group meetings for the whole ward, which I had begun soon after taking over. I was working, as far as possible within the existing hospital hierarchy, on the principles of the therapeutic community. There was open sharing of information; nursing staff were encouraged to discuss patients within the group rather than in their absence (see Chapters 9 and 11).

The multiple family therapy group was composed of patients and their families. Since the turnover on the ward was fairly rapid, it was run as a very open one, all families of ward patients being invited to join. Families were given to understand that commitment to regularity was important. It was impressed on parents that both should attend every session – a rule which, as we shall see, was not obvious to them.

If necessary, family group therapy was extended beyond the period of hospitalization; families were invited to continue on an outpatient basis after discharge. Bowen (1964) hospitalized the whole family with the patient. This would not have been acceptable to our families. We did, however, keep the family together, when this was feasible, by treating the identified patient as a day patient.

Meetings took place once every two weeks (which was found the most practicable) and lasted for an hour and a half. Most of our families had never heard of family therapy, certainly not of a family therapy group; I did not expect specific motivation to attend such a group, but used their motive force. Families had various expectations of the therapist, conscious and unconscious: reassurance, relief from anxiety and guilt feelings, possibly a magic 'cure' for the identified patient that would turn her into just the kind of person they wanted without any need for change on their part. The tension in the family can thus be used as motive force. Support given to individual family members tends to reduce the tension and is therefore counterproductive. Bowen's (1964) practice of hospitalizing whole families increased anxiety and was more effective for that reason.

Nursing staff were instructed that anyone asking to see me be directed to the family group; whatever they had to say should be said in the group. This meant that families could join the group without screening or selection; selection was through the group process. Some families could not survive it and dropped out, while others who had originally been reluctant became active and enthusiastic participants. (I did take a family history from families who brought the patient.)

The group was intentionally heterogeneous, both as regards family composition and diagnosis. The attending family members could be the spouses of a patient, or the parents (and siblings, when possible). The diagnosis could be schizophrenia, bipolar illness, character disorder or severe neurosis. This heterogeneity was an advantage. The mother of a boy with character disorder might point out the absurdity in the attitude of the mother of a schizophrenic woman. The healthy daughter of a couple with marital problems might compare her relationship with her parents to that of a schizophrenic in the group.

We sometimes allowed a patient to attend whose family would not. They were keen participants and worked at making vicarious amendment of the family rift in the group.

> Ex. 10(i). Diane aged 23, came from a broken home; her parents never visited and seemed to take no interest in her. She had been diagnosed as antisocial personality disorder. She had asked permission to join the group and was given it. In the group, she surprised everyone by her empathic understanding. She understood how parents felt about their children and gave attending parents some idea of how it felt to be a young person in hospital. Diane had a need to care for others, to 'make reparation', and thereby to vicariously care for herself. She had fantasies of having a baby of her own whom she could love. Her role in the group was a nurturant one. It seemed also to have a healing effect on her.

The group process

Being a compound group, the group process may be said to have several dimensions: intra-family (Dimension One), intra-group (Dimension Two), and between group and therapists (Dimension Three). The intrapsychic dimension, in so far as it enters the picture, can be designated Zero Dimension. Dimensions and perspectives can be represented in a chart (Figure 10.1).

Dimension	Interaction	Perspectives
0	Intrapsychic	e.g. Patient on himself, mother on herself
1	Intra-family	Each family member's view of every other member, e.g. mother considers son vulnerable, father considers him spoilt, son regards mother as weak
2	Intra-group: between families; between the patient and his/her family; between the patient and the member of another family	Group on a family; group on individual family member; patient on a family; patient on the member of another's family
3	Between group and therapist	Group on therapist (including transference); therapist on an individual (e.g. family member); therapist on a family; therapist on interaction between the patient and a family; therapist on group as a whole; therapist on his/her relation to group (countertransference)

Figure 10.1 Dimentions and perspectives of the multiple family therapy group.

Let us look at the dimensions of the group space. In the case of the group of individuals, we are particularly interested in intra-group relating, in what happens between group members. (Dimension Three here, Dimension Two in the individual's group). We consider that it reflects the way the group member relates to significant others in life outside the group. This includes relations of the GM with his family.

In the case of the multiple family therapy group, the family is before us. We can see what happens between family members. What we see may not be the whole picture, and possibly a distorted one; we cannot, after all, be a fly on the wall in the family home. Yet it does give us a fair idea of how family members relate to one another. We are therefore particularly interested in the intra-familial dimension (Dimension One) of the multiple family group.

Dimension Two has its own interest. It gives an unaccustomed space to group members. The mother of one boy can be a different kind of mother to someone else's child. The only child can get a taste of what it is like to have siblings.

We could be led to conclude that because of the importance of the intra-family dimension, the therapist should largely focus on this dimension. Yet there are good reasons to leave this work to the group, at least in the first instance. One reason is the problem of partiality. The other concerns unique and shared perspectives.

Let us begin with the latter. If we look at the perspectives in Figure 10.1, we can see that other group members, other families, have a perspective on the intra-family dimension (D1). On the other hand, the therapist is the only one who has a perspective on the group as a whole, and everything that goes on in the space of Dimension Two. If the therapist interprets what happens within a family, there is no advantage over single family therapy. We would not be making the most of the group's potential to make observations in this dimension.

As to partiality, the therapist may be drawn into taking the part of one family member rather than another. If she has been treating the identified patient all along, she might well see the family from the patient's point of view. Even if she is not biased, she may be perceived as being so. (The therapist is usually perceived by the family as the agent of the family member she has been treating.) Thus, there is much to be said for leaving observations in this dimension to be made by group members, at least in the first instance. If indicated, the therapist may enlarge on or comment on group members' observations.

Transference interpretations are less important in the group than in individual therapy, and less important in the family therapy group than in the group of individuals. One reason is this: in individual therapy, transference interpretations serve to reflect what is happening in the here-and-now of the therapy and are virtually the only means of doing so. This function is adequately filled by here-and-now interpretation of events in the group which throw light on the group member's modes of relating to significant others. Since 'transference to the group' can be very clearly seen and reflected back to the GM, transference to the therapist is, on the whole, less important. We need draw attention to it only when it is important to do so in the interest of the group process. (In the case of the family therapy group, this means rarely.)

As mentioned above, interaction within each family is easily observable in the group. Unlike many couples, whose inclination is not to wash their dirty linen in public, families of schizophrenics tend to display characteristic ways of interacting in the group. In fact, we found that families showed much cohesion, with so much esoteric communication among themselves that they were unable to relate to the group. It was as if all their valencies were taken up by themselves and none were left free for bonding with other group members, other families or the group as a whole. (Hence the rule that families were not to sit together.)

Perspectives

A family cannot see itself as a whole, in perspective. A member of a family is, similarly, unable to see the family's relating to him in perspective.

Other group members, and the group as a whole, had a good perspective on each family, and, indeed, often made pertinent observations. Such observations might be made by patients or healthy family members.

The task of the therapist is to encourage and empower the group to work. Thus, the group can be left to make observations on individuals and on families. The therapist need intervene only when the group is stuck. Just as a patient in a group of individuals can make interpretations, it was found that a patient might make interpretations about another family.

Multiple therapists

As was the principle on the ward, nursing staff and occupational therapists were encouraged to take part in the group, though they were not always active participants. Beyond this, co-therapy or multiple therapy is very useful in groups composed of families (as it is in couples groups). A single therapist easily finds himself drawn into siding with a particular family member. He may be perceived as siding with one family member even if he is not, particularly if he has had previous contact with that family member. One way is to allow the group to comment on this dimension in the first instance (see above). Another is to make use of a second (or third) therapist, who is probably in a position to recognize such bias and to neutralize it.

When family members manipulate one therapist into a specific involvement, another is emotionally free to interpret it. The policy is to allow freedom of expression, too. Though therapists often support and reinforce one another, it is permissible for one therapist to differ from the other if one feels that the other therapist has made a mistaken interpretation or is leading the group process in an undesirable direction. This freedom to differ models the permissibility of parents having differences of opinion. This is a thing much feared by the parents of schizophrenics, who believe that they must not argue in front of the children.

The danger is not contradiction, but overactivity. If one therapist deliberately refrains from intervening and the other is highly active, there is little the first can do. The therapists may be drawn into competing, which is unhelpful. Discussion after the meeting may minimize these problems. Each therapist is perceived differently in the transference at any point in time. For example, the psychiatrist (of either sex) may be perceived as the powerful, threatening father, while the social worker may be seen as the good, giving mother. This can be utilized: a particular therapist may be most effective when not playing the expected role.

Co-therapy also opens up the possibility of in-service training. We found there was always a great demand on the part of staff and students, as well as visitors, to observe the family therapy group or learn about it. We welcomed such students and observers though we kept an eye on the balance between patients and therapists/observers.

Manoeuvres in the service of resistance

One encounters resistance in all kinds of groups, but more so in the case of families of schizophrenics. They are likely to be afraid of upsetting the delicate balance they have found, keeping anxiety at a minimum. What is more, they did not ask to come for treatment as a family. On the other hand, most of them are aghast at the crisis in the identified patient that led to admission and are willing 'to do anything to help'. Some families have reason to feel relief at this admission, but then their guilt feelings at the relief may lead them to cooperate.

We noticed a number of phenomena specific to the multiple family therapy group, including making the family impermeable. It was found that families seated themselves together, with a great deal of intra-familial communication, mostly esoteric (private language, whispering, gestures and body language). This tended to make the family into a self-contained and impermeable unit. Neither the family nor the individuals composing it could communicate with others in the group. I therefore made it a rule for family members not to sit together. As might be expected, there was still some characteristic intra-familial communication; preventing a family member from speaking, or superfluously 'giving permission' to speak. But this was now open and obvious and could be commented on or interpreted if necessary.

The alternating parent phenomenon

Parents could of course resist by not attending the group at all. However, it was possible to appear cooperative and attend, but never both parents at the same time. My impression was that this was due to unconscious fear that conflict between the spouses would come out into the open. Again, there might be fear of disturbing the dynamic equilibrium in the family. They sensed such disturbance would occur if the whole family attended.

Defences based on the use of language

The family might communicate with one another in a language not understood by the rest of the group, in esoteric phraseology or in gestures. A family member might attempt to speak to the therapist in a language not understood by the identified patient. This is akin to discussing her in her absence, though here it is clear to the patient that a communication about her is being made and there is thus less mystification.

Group members may speak to one another in a language not understood by the rest of the group. (This is prominent in a country of immigrants like Israel.)

Competing with the therapist

Parents might compete with the therapist, or compete with hospital staff, as to who is the better mother.

> Ex. 10(ii). Mrs Green's 30-year-old daughter Minna was a very sick chronic schizophrenic who was reluctant to do anything, even to eat. Mrs Green would ask Minna to sit next to her in group meetings. If she did not, she accused her of not loving her mother.
>
> Mrs Green would complain that the staff was not looking after Minna properly, and that only she saw to it that Minna ate, washed or performed her excretory functions. She would inspect Minna for cleanliness when she came to visit. At most visits she brought food, and would spoon-feed Minna or watch while she ate. On certain days Minna refused the hospital lunch on the grounds that her mother was coming. Mrs Green's need to be the feeding mother thus came to be fulfilled.
>
> One might add, in retrospect, that Minna was one of the patients who showed little improvement following family group therapy.

Manifestations of the pathological family process in the group

Invalidating the patient's communications

Family members have various ways of silencing the identified patient. All invalidate his words and threaten his autonomy.

SILENCING DIRECTLY

As soon as the identified patient ventures an opinion, a family member tells him, verbally or by gesture, to shut up. The implication is that, being sick, he will make a fool of himself, or that children should be seen and not heard. If a member of another family is talking, they intimate that it is 'not nice' to mind another's business. The effect is to bind the patient to the family, blocking his individuation. Since according to the group culture everyone minds everyone's business, other group members may tell these parents they are wrong.

ANSWERING IN THE IDENTIFIED PATIENT'S PLACE

When the patient is asked a question, the parent answers instead. The implication is that 'the child' cannot reply, needs protection, or his reply is unreliable. He is not a person in his own right. The device also copes with the anxiety that the patient might reveal something the family wants to keep secret.

MEDIATING

Mediating is more subtle. The family member gives permission to the patient to answer, implying that permission is required: 'Answer the question' or 'Tell the doctor about it'. There may be aggression in the injunction ('Why don't you answer?'), when all along it is the family member who has been preventing the patient from doing so. (This usually happens after it has repeatedly been pointed out to the family member that he or she is answering in the patient's place.) There may be a broad hint at the direction the answer is to take ('Tell the doctor how good you felt at home').

The phenomenon is similar to the domination of a therapy group by a manic patient. When this monopolization is pointed out to her, she does the rounds in giving permission to speak. She is still dominating the group, though overtly complying with the request to give way.

Other ways of impeding group communication

As in all groups, members of family groups may have characteristic ways of impeding free communication. A common way is to talk but leave no space for response. A family member may describe a problem or reiterate a question, ignoring the fact that all along another group member is trying to answer it or relate to it. This may reflect their mode of communicating in the family.

There may be selective inattention: responses are made possible but simply not heard by a particular group member, who goes on as if the response had not been made.

Misinterpreting the significance of change

Change in the identified patient, of whatever kind, is often perceived as a threat to the family, who fear a disturbance of the family equilibrium. The simplest example is the anxiety felt by the family of the bipolar patient at signs of activity.

The family (whether spouse or parents) have learnt to fear the manifestations of manic cycles and prefer the patient slightly depressed.

The family of a schizophrenic may feel threatened at signs of initiative and activity in the patient. Rather than perceive them as signs of differentiation and individuation, they may interpret them as illness. Here is an example.

> Ex. 10(iii). Mrs Brown says that Joseph is 'getting nervous' again. He now works until 7 p.m. The employer tells her the social worker agreed. (Joseph, aged 17, is working, for the first time in his life, as an apprentice carpenter.) Joseph retorts that he ought to be paid for these hours. Another group member suggests that he look for another job; Joseph declines.
>
> Mrs Brown complains that Joseph is getting angry with her, taking it out on her. He ought to tell his employer what he thinks. Joseph is complaining that his shirts are not properly washed; he has never done such a thing before.
>
> The therapist remarks that Mrs Brown is unused to Joseph being angry, but it is natural. Edna remarks that her boys are like this all the time. Reena says that this is what boys are like. Mrs Brown reiterates that Joseph has never said anything like this before. Her husband never complains. Reena remarks: 'You now have two men in the house, not one.'
>
> Mrs Brown remarks: 'I used to bring everything to Joseph in the morning. Now he is up at six, jumps out of bed. He calls his brother, "up you get". I think he is getting nervous again.'
>
> We note that the mother perceives Joseph's complaining as sick, and even more oddly, his rising in the morning on his own initiative. Requiring help in dressing is perceived as normal.

Facilitative and mutative functions of the group

One could divide the therapeutic functions of the group into facilitative and mutative, though in practice it is not always easy to distinguish them. The facilitative function includes facilitating expression of emotion, improvement of communication, removing mystification. Under mutative functions we could discuss interpretations, and the advantages of interpretations made by group members, which are often more acceptable to other group members than those made by the therapist. As we shall see, the improved communication in itself turns out to be therapeutic.

The facilitating function of the group: facilitating the expression of emotion

Families of schizophrenics tend to have difficulty in expressing emotion. They deny hate and anger, blur negative feelings, avoid any expression of feelings that might lead to conflict. Such parents may lack warm feelings for their child and may feel ambivalent towards them. They may love them as if they were part of themselves rather than persons in their own right, a part-object as opposed to a whole-object love. (This fits in with the theory that parents of schizophrenics are themselves not highly differentiated.) Not only are such negative emotions not expressed, but also they may not reach awareness.

The disparity between what the parent expresses and what he really feels is sensed by the child. At best it makes him distrust his own judgement about the feelings of others. At worst, the constant invalidation of his assessment drives him crazy.

Ackerman holds that intrapsychic conflict must be activated and reprojected into the field of family interaction if a healthful soultion is to be found (Ackerman 1961).

Encouraging the expression of negative feelings leads to stormy sessions which may be frightening to the group, possibly even the therapist. In the case of the Brown family, overt hate was expressed.

> Ex. 10(iv). Joseph had been admitted to our unit at 17, schizophrenic, behaving childishly and apparently inaccessible to verbal or activity therapy. This is the history of the family.
>
> Mr and Mrs Brown are both Holocaust survivors. Mr Brown had lost his own mother when he was 7, and at 15 had been interned in a concentration camp where he witnessed the death of his father and sister.
>
> As an infant, Joseph was pampered by his mother and his grandmother. He was a stubborn baby: when he did not get his way, he had breath-holding attacks which frightened his mother into giving him what he wanted. Mrs Brown aborted one pregnancy because of Joseph's jealousy on discovering it. The next time she took care to tell Joseph early. Soon after the birth of Joseph's brother, his grandmother died. He threatened suicide by jumping from a balcony and was admitted to a psychiatric hospital. There were several admissions before he came to us.
>
> Mrs Brown told us that she continued to give Joseph all he asked for. If frustrated he would behave wildly. In group meetings, she sometimes asked Joseph whether he loved her, and if he loved her more than his father.
>
> Mr Brown came only after some persuasion. In his first month in the group, he shocked the group by stating his belief that all mentally ill people should be killed. When questioned he replied that this would include his son, if there were no hope for him. He frequently reiterated that he was afraid of nothing; fear was a weakness. He regarded family relations as a battle ground, where giving was a weakness.
>
> These forthright declarations of hate seemed eventually to lead to good things. Sixteen months after admission, Mr Brown arranged for Joseph to be appren-

ticed to a carpenter, and the boy held down a job for the first time in his life. The family was asked to continue in the group as outpatients, but defaulted until problems arose again.

In the later stages of therapy the picture changed. The father still spoke of 'doing something for which he might get life imprisonment', if Joseph became angry, this time as an impulse of which he was afraid. Two years after admission, Joseph heard his father declare his affection for him, and was clearly very happy about it.

Interpreting the symptom: translating non-verbal interaction

As in all groups with psychotic members, it is important to understand symptom language and translate it into interpersonal language. This is best illustrated with an example.

> Ex. 10(v). Aliza, 23, had been admitted in severe depression, after suicidal threats. She had left home but was unable to cope on her own. She complained that she had never been loved as much as her siblings; moreover, she was backward and ashamed of it. She felt she was different from her friends. (We found below-average intelligence and specific dyslexia. She had been referred to a special school, but her father, though a school principal, had refused to let her take this up.)

At first, Aliza refused to attend the groups. She worried the staff by refusing to eat more than the bare minimum. At times she asked leave to go out and kill herself. 'My parents have a good-for-nothing [daughter], I'll show them.'

Having improved somewhat, Aliza began to ask to go home for weekends. Her mother now complained of a new symptom: Aliza vomited while at home (though not in hospital). The mother guessed this was psychogenic but did not know how to deal with it. She was invited to join the family group together with her daughter.

When the subject of Aliza's vomiting arose, I explained that Aliza was beginning to accept her mother, but could not do so wholeheartedly. Her request to come home signified acceptance, her vomiting rejection. Aliza found this hard to say in words. The interpretation was repeated the next session. The mother told us that she was nonetheless worried and would coax Aliza to drink. I remarked that Aliza seemed to enjoy the spoiling that did not come to her in any other way. She seemed to require proof that her mother loved her sufficiently to worry about her. Care was taken not to put pressure on Aliza to give up the symptom before she was ready.

After a third family group, Aliza was told in her individual session: 'I wonder if you have the willpower not to be sick at home.' She vomited that weekend, but not the next, and there was no recurrence when Aliza enjoyed longer leaves.

Removing mystification

'Protecting' a child through withholding important information is a form of mystification. In some cases it leads to psychosis.

> Ex. 10(vi). Anthony, a schoolboy in his last class in grammar school, was
> admitted in a borderline state with severe anxiety and suicidal thoughts. His
> elder brother had committed suicide ten years earlier after a psychotic
> breakdown. His parents had kept this a secret from him; his mother told him that
> he had died of influenza. Only later, when Anthony spoke of suicide, his mother
> burst out: 'But your brother killed himself.'

> In a joint session, Anthony explained that he had not believed his brother was
> dead; he thought he might be in the secret service. He realized, retrospectively,
> that he had sensed something false about his mother's account of his brother's
> dying of an illness. His problem was that he could not trust anyone.

> In the family group, the mother continued to speak of the elder boy's illness. The
> therapist persuaded her that this mystification was causing her son more
> confusion and anxiety than an admission of the painful truth. The facts were
> then adequately clarified.

> Anthony recovered within a few weeks and continued psychotherapy as an
> outpatient. He was well enough to be accepted for regular army service.

Acceptability of interpretations by group members

In any group, interpretations made by fellow group members tend to be accepted
more easily, arouse less resistance, than those made by the conductor. Group
members are 'one of us' while the therapist represents authority.

In the multiple family therapy group, observations on the family structure were
more acceptable when made by other group members, usually the children of
other families. The fact that they were patients did not make them any less valid in
the eyes of those observed.

> Ex. 10(vii). Eric was a bachelor living with his widowed father. The father was
> saying that he wished Eric would manage his money better. He wished that he
> would work, be more autonomous. Eric retorted that he had been earning
> money through private tutoring. The trouble was that his father would not let
> him go. The group explored the relationship between father and son, and
> revealed that it was a very close, symbiotic one (cf. Ex. 9(iv)).

Foulkes (1948, pp.120 ff.) has written about unconscious understanding, in the
case of groups with neurotic patients. This is an important factor in the case of
groups of psychotic patients, who freely associate to the conscious or unconscious
ideas of others. This is something the therapist has to bear in mind when seeking

connection between apparently unconnected material. It may also lead to appropriate interpretations by group members.

> Ex. 10(viii). Mrs L. complained that her son was indifferent to all she did for him; he even scorned her cooking. Mrs S. replied: 'More than the calf wants to suck, the cow wants to suckle.' Mrs S. had recently given birth and the metaphor behind this common saying was very real for her. At that point, however, it was the perfect interpretation: hitting the nail on the head, and giving the message that Mrs L. was not alone in what she felt.

Mirroring and vicarious learning

Foulkes (1964) defines mirror reactions as:

> characteristically brought-out when a number of persons meet and interact. The person sees himself, or part of himself – often repressed part of himself – reflected in the interactions of other group members. He sees them reacting in the way he does himself, or in contrast to his own behaviour. He also gets to know himself – and this is a fundamental process in ego development – by the effect he has on others and the picture they form of him. (Foulkes 1964, p.110)

The first meaning of 'mirroring' is particularly important in group members who are reluctant to be actively involved, as is often the case with some families of patients. They can learn about themselves vicariously, without active participation.

> Ex. 10(ix). Mrs G. was the mother of Tony, a 17 year old who was in hospital under a court order after driving a bus without licence or authorization. She came under protest, proclaiming all along that she saw no point, and was rather passive in the group. When another family was arguing we suddenly found her intervening on behalf of the 19 year old: 'The boy must feel he is not wanted in the house.' Her face lit up with enthusiasm on finding herself involved. Later she took the part of the boy's mother.

We do not know how much any particular silent member benefits vicariously from the group, but there is reason to believe that they do learn by projective processes, by mirroring. My own experience on sitting in on a group suggests this.

Summary

The multiple family therapy group is a useful tool in the therapy of acute hospitalized schizophrenics, as well as patients suffering from bipolar disorders, dissociative states and possibly personality disorders. We found it particularly effective for those suffering from acute schizophrenia (from a few weeks' to a few years' duration), less so in some very chronic readmitted patients who were part of very enmeshed families or in symbiotic relationships. When, in some cases, individual sessions were given to families, we found that 'more' is not 'better'. The group itself is a potent instrument for change.

CHAPTER 11

The Case for the Therapeutic Community

The therapeutic community is an added dimension of the therapeutic group. We recall (Chapter 2) that we saw the dyad of individual therapy as having a single, linear dimension. The group is two-dimensional. The therapeutic community is three-dimensional. Although the whole community is not always present at any point in time, it is constantly present in the therapeutic space. Foulkes (1948, p.32) represents dimensions as concentric circles: the innermost is self-analysis, the next psychoanalysis, the third is group analysis. Circle 4 is 'open air psychiatry' and circle 5 is 'life'. As an example of circle 4 he gives a group of soldiers working at a carpentry project at Northfields, England, which was in fact the first therapeutic community.

Whiteley (1999) calls the therapeutic community a continuous large group. When an institution is not a therapeutic community, there is likelihood of discordance between the small group and the 'large group' of all those administering the institution. Maxwell Jones, pioneer of the hospital therapeutic community, was aware of the difficulty. He writes (1968, p.41): 'We would certainly go so far as to say that these skills [i.e. those of the psychiatrist] employed, say, in group treatment, may be rendered largely ineffective if the social climate of the hospital as a whole is opposed to such a form of treatment.'

This discordance is at the root of the difficulty of conducting groups on a long-stay ward, the emptiness of content towards which they tend, and the often depressing countertransference feelings of the therapists of such groups.

Main (1946), another of the pioneers of the therapeutic community, defines it as:

> an attempt to use a hospital not as an organization run by doctors in the interests of their own greater technical efficiency, but as a community with the immediate

aim of full participation of all its members in its daily life and the eventual aim of resocialization of the neurotic individual for life in ordinary society. (Main 1946, p.67)

The nature of the therapeutic community orientation

The essential features of the therapeutic community have been enumerated as democratization, communalism, permissiveness and reality confrontation (Rapoport 1960). The specific feature, however, the one that makes all the difference, is democratization, the sharing of responsibility with patients. This means not only a structural revolution but also a psychological upheaval for the therapist. Surrendering both authority and benign paternalism, the professional has to rely on personal qualities, to meet the patient as a person and be exposed to the distress that this brings about. It requires conviction, perhaps a leap of faith. It may be most difficult for the psychiatrist, who has to doff his white coat literally and metaphorically. In one workshop on groups, a psychologist from the Upper Galilee said he admired me for 'giving up being a psychiatrist' and engaging with groups. The nurse, too, working in a less authoritative manner, may feel uncomfortable at first. However, in Laing's early experiment at Gartnavel, having chronic patients meet each day with the same nurse, nurses had 'initially intensive mixed feelings and insecurities,' but later felt 'more involved and related to patients' (Andrews 1998, p.127).

The staff of therapeutic communities do not only have to undergo personal change; they have to solve recurrent dilemmas of responsibility. Legally and morally they are still responsible, though the patient is given as much autonomy as possible.

The immediacy of involvement with the patient's suffering is often difficult, particularly in the case of psychotic and borderline patients. The therapist must also be prepared to receive the patient's projections. 'What I found disquieting is that a student is not only a giver of love and attention, but also a container of anger and depression... At the beginning I felt persecuted by this and only later did I realize that this was an important function.' Thus Irene Bruna Seu, a student at an Arbours Community (Berke, Masoliver and Ryan 1995, p.34).

On the same subject, Berke writes on discussion about a difficult 'guest' (as patients are called there):

> We seemed to get increasingly acrimonious in our relationships with each other... Then it occurred to me that this sense of intense pressure we felt, and were inflicting on each other, was to do with the very tensions this man was suffering. He was not able to communicate them directly, but he chose to communicate and to get rid of the pressures by arousing them in us... As soon as we appreciated this, the tensions in us became manageable. We didn't need to interpret this to him. (Berke et al. 1995, p.67)

Motivation

Foulkes created the first therapeutic community in an army hospital at Northfields during the Second World War. He describes how, in the earlier setting, soldiers regarded their symptoms as a means of discharge from the army. By actively involving soldiers in the running of the unit and hence in their treatment, Foulkes created motivation. Whatever had been the soldiers' secondary gain from their illness, they had now become interested in becoming fit and useful citizens.

Another area in which lack of motivation is a problem is in the treatment of personality disorders which are egosyntonic. The effect on motivation might well be one of the key factors which makes the therapeutic community for personality disorders, as developed by Maxwell Jones, so effective. (There is a policy not to receive offenders on a court order, but only those who had already run their sentence. Treatment must be voluntarily sought.)

Development of autonomous morality through the therapeutic community

Piaget (1932) shows that in the early years, a child learns to obey her parents, without being able to give reasons. She internalizes parental authority. Later, in the peer group, she acquires a sense of fairness and is able to give reasons for her moral actions. She also acts in a concerned and compassionate manner. Piaget calls these phases 'morality of duty' and 'morality of love'.

Money-Kyrle (1952) classifies morality into two kinds: superego morality and humanist morality. The former is based on obedience to authority, external or internalized, the latter on compassion and concern, and loyalty to personal values. There seems to be a parallel in Piaget's and Money-Kyrle's two moralities. (See the more detailed discussion in Chapter 14.)

In the therapeutic community, too, peer group relationships are emphasized. Moreover, patients are given responsibility for the running of the community and thus learn to work out rules for themselves. They themselves discover what is fair and what is not. One would expect the therapeutic community to further the development of autonomous morality, and this is what one sees happening. On visiting the Henderson Hospital, a therapeutic community in Surrey for personality disorders, in 1983, I was struck by the way residents were not afraid of criticizing staff, including the superintendent. It was residents who took on a moral role, a superego function. It was they who told the errant alcoholic to stop drinking. In the Internal Rehabilitation Unit near Jerusalem, it was a resident who held that attendance at the morning group should be compulsory, and suggested a way of implementing this. (See below, this chapter.)

Gil Elles, a psychoanalyst who worked at the Henderson, has a theory of moral development in the therapeutic community (Jones 1968, p.99.) First, the new patient is accepted for what he is, so that deep-seated guilt is relieved and ego-strength made more available. Second, since the patient is expected to give as well as receive treatment, he is eventually able 'to feel less threatened in admitting some part of his own desperation about himself'. Third, through the various groups, he is able to see a more integrated picture of himself.

> Thus some patients for the first time experience both an outer security and an inner despair which allows them to feel and to understand the emotions of remorse and pity, followed by a longing for and a belief in their own ability to repair and restore the fabric of damaged relationships. (Jones 1968, p.99)

The therapeutic community ideology in education: paternalism versus democratization

Professor Alice Shalvi (personal communication) introduced a democratic regime in the girls' grammar school in Jerusalem which she directed. A committee consisting of an equal number of staff and pupils was formed to deal with breaches of discipline and other problems. This taught the pupils to form their own judgement on moral issues. It enabled them to gain perspective on the school as a whole as well as being able to empathize with the individual pupil.

The aim here was frankly educational, developing a sense of responsibility and autonomous morality. There seems to be a similar line of thought here to the responsibility sharing in the therapeutic community.

The therapeutic community with schizophrenics

The therapeutic community for schizophrenics has a history, associated both with 'anti-psychiatry' and revolutions within psychiatric hospitals (which are not so different). Laing, who founded Kingsley Hall in London, did not perceive schizophrenia as an illness, so that there were no patients and no doctors. David Cooper, who initiated 'Villa 21' in Shenley Hospital near London, was the first to use milieu therapy for acute schizophrenia (Pullen 1999, pp.368–369). 'Villa 21' was a therapeutic community with morning community meetings, small groups and work groups. As to revolutions within the system, Clark (1974) was a pioneer, Martin (1962) was another. Pullen (1999) gives an excellent account, both of the history and of his own involvement with the therapeutic community in schizophrenia. However, the approach is still not widely accepted.

Two main questions arise with regard to the therapeutic community with schizophrenics (and other mentally ill patients): first, is it possible? Second, is it necessary?

Can we share responsibility with schizophrenics?

It may be argued that judgement is impaired in psychosis, certainly in the acute phase, if not throughout. Schizophrenics might act on their delusions. There are depressives who do not want to live; we protect them from themselves until they recover from their depression. Thus we may have doubts about sharing responsibility with mentally ill patients.

In practice, it is possible and desirable to give them as much responsibility as they can bear. Consider two cases.

> Ex. 11(i). (See also Ex. 9(ix).) Aaron was in his fifties, divorced with no children. He had been in the police force before falling ill and was discharged after a violent act against a colleague. Later, he had found his wife in bed with a lover. He had refrained from using the gun he was carrying, but threw the lover out of the balcony. Aaron lived alone when he joined the group, lonely yet unable to bear company. His family had rejected him except for his mother, who frequently invited him for weekends. Even then, when his young nephews and nieces were present, he could not bear the noise and would shut himself in a room in his mother's house.

When Aaron's mother was dying, the family had her sign a will that excluded him on the grounds of being mentally unfit. Not unexpectedly, he was extremely angry and often spoke of this in the group. The will was later found to be invalid and required his agreement. He decided that he would never sign: let them have nothing even if he had nothing. When the family made overtures towards his reconciliation, he discussed this in the group. The consensus was that they merely wanted their money. Aaron resolved that he would certainly not go to their weddings after they had cut him off for so long. His anger smouldered undiminished. Fortunately there was a family member who still cared for him; an uncle living in Canada, who invited him once or twice a year, paying all expenses.

When Aaron first joined the group, he was extremely self-centred and demanding. In one session, after the group had discussed his problems for half an hour and moved on to other matters, he declared: 'No one is taking any notice of me, I shall burn myself to death.' This was not untypical. Slowly he learnt to relate to what others were saying, understanding the principle of reciprocity.

While Aaron's mother was still alive, there was an incident in which he had become angry in her house, smashing a bottle with his foot and also breaking the small bones of the foot. His sister demanded his hospitalization. My co-therapist and I decided that we would have him sign an agreement: he would undertake not to be violent towards himself or towards others, on pain of hospitalization.

Aaron took his promise very seriously. He once told us how a man had insulted him on a bus. 'I wanted to hit him, but I remembered the undertaking in my pocket and refrained.'

After the family's rejection, he was extremely angry and spoke of burning down their houses. The group did much to calm him, but, as he told us, the undertaking also helped. Anger was channelled into the group dialogue, and always remained verbal, despite Aaron's existential difficulties.

Aaron was diagnosed schizophrenia simplex. He was of below average intelligence, and his whole life had been characterized by violent incidents. Nonetheless, we entrusted him with some responsibility for controlling his violence and he stood up to it.

Schizophrenics can help one another.

Ex. 11(ii). Paul was in his forties and single; he had been diagnosed paranoid schizophrenia and had spent years in hospital before being rehabilitated to a hostel. I had in fact known him for some years; I knew he had a rich inner life. He had spoken of himself as a ship on a stormy sea while still in hospital. In the Rehabilitation Unit he had produced imaginative paintings. He would often ask why he could not go home. 'I work, I take my medication, I am not violent.' At that time, the policy was not to discharge anyone to their family. When there was a policy change, he was considered suitable for rehabilitation in a town flat. He became a member of our outpatient group.

In the group sessions, Paul frequently related to the problems of others, making constructive suggestions, though he had a tendency to manic denial, making things more rosy than they were. He himself was content, had no problems. Once in two or three months he would suddenly mumble incomprehensively and with no connection to the context of the dialogue. He appeared to be psychotic, and this was clear to the group members as well as the therapists. At such times he refused additional medication with an aggressiveness untypical of him. The next thing we would hear was that his family were taking him to hospital. After a week or two, he would be released with a long-acting drug by injection. He asked if he could discontinue this, and was put on a long-acting drug by mouth. This kept him on an even keel – until the next time.

One day Paul asked if he might come off all medication. 'I have been in the group for eight years, have taken my medication. I think I no longer need it. I want to try and do without it. I shall go on coming to the group.'

The group tried to dissuade him. Tom, who himself had periodic breakdowns, explained that one did not know, could not recognize when one was going crazy. I was in a dilemma (and it was I, as the psychiatrist, who had to decide). On the one hand, Paul was rational and making a reasonable request. On the other hand, I knew that in the past he had had sudden attacks of psychosis in which he was not accessible. I decided that, on ethical grounds, I ought to grant his request. I asked him to sign a statement that he was doing this at his own risk and against medical advice.

My co-therapist and the nurse observer applauded my decision. However, I trembled.

The following week, Paul told the group: 'I went back to my medication. I found I needed it, I was not feeling good without it.' We were surprised and pleased.

The interesting thing was that since the incident Paul was much more realistic in his contributions to the group dialogue. It seems that giving him responsibility for his medication had increased his self-esteem, and in some way helped him get his feet on the ground. There was less rosy idealization and more down-to-earth judgement.

Sometimes patients use their illness to evade responsibility for their actions, for example, in family relationships.

Ex. 11(iii). Shira is divorced, living with a steady boyfriend. She has a son and a daughter by her marriage; the daughter has a baby son. Her relationship with her children is good, but she tends to exploit the fact of her illness in various ways. She expects her daughter to coddle her when she is depressed, while in fact making her miserable with her complaints. When she describes this situation in a group session, usually in a whining tone, the group is asked how it makes them feel. We show her that this kind of behaviour is counterproductive.

Conversely, she visits her grandson when in a hyperactive state and apparently behaves inappropriately, according to her daughter. 'I can't help it, I am not responsible,' she tells the group. I point out that she is quite capable of taking responsibility. 'But it is my right to be not responsible – I am sick.'

Shira has been diagnosed as bipolar disorder. We find, also, that she has the self-centredness of the immature personality. Our aim in the group is to help her take responsibility for herself and to learn to see the other's point of view.

These examples illustrate that schizophrenic and bipolar patients are able to take on responsibility in certain areas when they are credited with the ability to do so, even in areas problematic for them. What is more, patients who are not able to help themselves in specific areas can nonetheless help other group members with their problems. This may be because their own experience helped them overcome some problems the others are battling with. It may also be because they are strong in areas in which others are weak. In our group, Bernie was always able to advise Deborah on bringing up her little girl. He had raised six children himself. He also knew how it felt to lose one's temper and want to hit a child. He too was beaten in his own childhood and knew how destructive it was.

But personal experience is not the only explanation. Sidney, who had never had children, gave some valid advice to Daniel and Deborah on the question of what to do when he came home from work. He was tired, wanting a rest; his little girl wanted to play. On one occasion he had slapped her when he went to rest. It was Sidney who suggested that he put his feet up for ten minutes or so, and then spend some time playing with his daughter. This was acceptable to the couple.

Bernie, on the other hand, was hypersensitive to rejection. He had lived alone since his divorce. His married daughter had been inviting him to dinner at weekends. After two such meals he backed off, fearing he might be a burden on her husband. The group listened with chagrin and tried to get him to see things differently – an aim not achievable in a single session. Bernie would rather decline an offer than lay himself open to refusal, rejection. Group members knew only too well that the healthy had 'no time for us' (the mentally ill). Their gentle efforts to strengthen Bernie's self-esteem may have had some effect over time. When he had been physically ill, later, he accepted his sister's offer to stay with her for a week.

The need for the therapeutic community for acutely mentally ill people

The therapeutic community is important in the treatment of the acute schizo-phrenic for a number of reasons: to avoid the trauma of admission, in the sense of being forcibly taken away from one's home; to help the patient make sense of the illness, to give space to psychological treatment.

The trauma of admission

The therapeutic community is important in avoiding the trauma of forcible admission, which may be used as a means of isolating him from the community and the family, of protecting others from him. Rather, the patient is to be perceived as a person in crisis who requires intensive care and treatment. In Jerusalem, Dr Dov Friedlander of the Hebrew University Health Services (personal communication) once devised a form of 'home hospitalization', in which two students would look after a student who had become acutely psychotic: one to be with him, the other to shop and run errands. In Britain, the Arbours Crisis Centres deal excellently with persons in crisis: they provide shelter, a peer group of similar others, a structure of therapy hours, group meetings and resident therapists who are always there for them. The person is not called 'patient' (with its connotation of passivity), but 'guest'. There is concern only with dynamic assessment and understanding, not with diagnosis.

Making sense of the illness and integrating it into one's experience

There are two schools of thought: one which advises the person who has been ill to 'forget all about it', the other which recommends making sense of the illness and integrating it into one's experience. 'Forgetting it' is associated with traumatic admission, heavy medication and psychiatrists who regard the patient's communi-cations as nothing more than symptoms pointing to a diagnosis, not meaningful. 'Making sense' involves understanding the person in crisis, hearing her expres-sions of distress, and helping her make sense of the crisis in the setting of her life.

The latter helps her recover as quickly as possible, and tends to prevent recurrence of a psychotic crisis in the future. When there is a biochemical component in the psychotic exacerbation, as in bipolar illness, 'making sense' can help the person recognize early signs of exacerbation in the future.

Giving space to psychological treatment

Psychotherapy and interpretation can be very effective in many cases of acute psychosis, including those diagnosed as schizophrenia, as I learnt from Dr R.D. Scott at Napsbury Hospital (personal communication). The therapeutic community can give space to psychological treatment. To illustrate this, let us look at a therapeutic community on an acute admission ward.

The ward was part of a Jerusalem hospital, with 32 beds, mixed sex, serving a catchment area that included part of Jerusalem, as well as the south, including Beersheba and Eilat. It also received tourists who became ill; this included many volunteers who had come to work on kibbutzim. The admission rate was ten to twelve weekly.

WARD GROUPS

Within a short time of becoming consultant in charge of the ward, I established ward groups, first thing in the morning, three times weekly, lasting for an hour. This required negotiation with nursing staff and occupational therapists. The thrice weekly represented a compromise with occupational therapy: since the morning was the productive time for the patients, the occupational therapist (OT) did not want this time to be diminished each day. The OT was invited and attended the group. Nursing staff were also invited, although it took a little time for them to realize that their presence was important; the nurse in charge and perhaps one other would attend.

Every patient was invited to attend. Very manic patients sometimes caused a problem by monopolizing or disturbing the meeting; occasionally they had to be asked to leave.

The group was a mixture of ward meeting and therapeutic group. Nursing staff were encouraged to discuss events that had occurred. One of my aims was transparency: I wanted problems to be discussed in the patients' presence rather than behind their backs. If a problem had arisen in the evening, we wanted to hear about it in the meeting. This open discussion would tend to reduce paranoid reactions. It also made the nurses regard themselves as more accountable. There were none of the kind of measures I had encountered in another hospital, where a patient had been tied to the bed for asking too many questions!

There seemed to be no reason for division into small groups, as the ward was not very large, and turnover was rapid. Moreover, there was an advantage in having everyone present to discuss events happening in the ward.

As a channel for requests regarding medication, weekend or longer leave, a notebook was organized for patients to register these: they could ask for weekend or other leave, or request changes in medication. This increased patients' sense of control over their lives.

I had inherited the ward as a locked one, a feature I thought unworthy of a modern admission ward. After some work with the staff, we decided to open the doors. No one ran away. The fact that the doors were open diminished the sense of being imprisoned and the need to escape. I believe that the only possible justification for locking doors is to protect confused and disoriented patients. Unfortunately, the open admission ward was too much for the hospital as a whole, and after two weeks we closed the doors again.

FAMILY INVOLVEMENT

Families would visit, often with requests to see the doctor. I would interview the family together with the patient. It soon became clear that there were tensions in the family which had become focused on the identified patient.

I wanted an efficient means of treating the patients through their families, and a multiple family therapy group was developed. All family members wanting to see the doctor were directed to the group. Our families were not sophisticated and had little motivation or understanding what family therapy might be. We used their needs to see the doctor as a motive force for attending the group, and this worked very well (see also Chapter 10).

TREATMENT VERSUS CONTAINMENT

Hinshelwood (1999, p.484) quotes Bott (1976) on the conflicting tasks of the mental hospital: treatment versus containment. Containment, again, is divided 'between custody (locking the disturbance away from family and the public) and asylum (locking the world away from the patient)'. Bott (1976) points to the tension between therapy and locking the patient away from the family. Intuitively, I dealt with these tensions by having families, patients and staff present in the same group, and allowing them to be expressed in its course. As to 'locking the patient away from the family', this is a step that confirms the focusing of family tensions on to one family member, the 'identified patient'. In my multiple family therapy group, I endeavoured to deal with these tensions, locating them once more in the family and thus helping the patient recover. (See also Chapter 10, particularly the example of Joseph.)

Examples of psychological treatment of acute schizophrenics

Ex. 11(iv). This is a case of psychotherapy in and by the group. Harry, a young man newly admitted, told us that he believed that everyone was acting a part: the patients were not really patients, the nurses not really nurses, the doctors not really doctors. Other group members told him that in their experience, this was not so: everyone was authentic. Harry gave up his delusions within two days, and was soon able to go home.

Ex. 11(v). This is an illustration of family therapy. Anthony, a high school boy, was acutely paranoid, with delusions of being in the secret service. The suicide of a brother had been concealed from him. In joint sessions with his mother, and in the multiple family therapy group, work was done to remove the mystification and Anthony's delusions very quickly disappeared. On follow-up, we found that he later did well in his studies and was fit enough to be recruited to the Israel Defence Forces.

It is also worth looking at the example of Joseph, in Chapter 10, Ex. 10(iii) and (iv).

Psychological and biochemical models of psychosis

On the face of it, it would seem that the therapeutic community might be recommended by adherents of a psychological theory of schizophrenia, though not the biochemical enthusiasts. There is a wide spectrum of views, from the entirely psychological to the entirely organic.

Laing and Kingsley Hall

R.D. Laing's (1960) early view on schizophrenia was that it was a defence against an untenable position; he was the first to describe the existential anxieties that assailed the schizoid. Later, he saw schizophrenia as an inner journey leading to self-healing, requiring only a protected environment. Hence the first therapeutic community for schizophrenics, Kingsley Hall, established after difficult birth pangs, run voluntarily by Laing, Morton Schatzman, Joseph Berke and others. There was no hierarchy and there were no rules. The famous Mary Barnes, a nurse previously diagnosed as schizophrenic, came there to regress, and did so, precariously, to early infancy. She was treated, without drugs, mostly in the sense of 'being with', by Joseph Berke and the team, and eventually emerged healthy, a writer and artist. Her therapy involved an investment of time and devotion so great as to be generally impracticable (Barnes and Berke 1971).

The Arbours Communities

Berke and Schatzman (Berke *et al.* 1995, p.xv), believing 'that a person in inner turmoil needs a stable, supportive external environment, rather than just a mirror of their internal state', founded the more structured Arbours Communities. In these, there is definite structure, therapy hours, house meetings; there are students, residents, supervisors. As in most therapeutic communities, 'guests' (as the patients are called) participate in running the household. Guests are perceived as persons in crisis and receive intensive psychotherapeutic care. This work requires special skills of the therapists, including the readiness to receive projections, to be emotionally involved, and yet retain the ability to think. Diagnostic labels are never used; on the other hand, the need for pharmacotherapy is not totally ignored.

The blessings of pharmacotherapy

The discovery of specific psychotropic drugs which began in the 1950s is not to be discounted. Chlorpromazine, 'Largactil', the first, was long used in surgery before its usefulness in calming psychotic excitement was discovered: it had none of the dangers of the barbiturates, nor the nastiness of paraldehyde, whose smell had pervaded wards until then. Until migraine was found to cause elation in the TB patients in which it was used, there was no treatment for depression. Leonard Woolf, in his autobiography, described his difficulties in treating Virginia's depressions, when she would refuse all food. All he could do was have her looked after in a nursing home and hope she would recover. Whether her tragic suicide, in a state of psychotic depression, would have been prevented by medication is of course a matter for speculation.

A conviction that pharmacotherapy is important in some cases of schizophrenia does not necessarily imply a belief in the organic origin of the condition. In my view, schizophrenia is more of a syndrome than a 'disease' with origins which can or should be definable. In some cases, it is easy to see disturbed family relations, in others, it is not. Sometimes, it is also possible to cure early cases of paranoid schizophrenia by psychotherapy or family therapy, as in the case of Anthony (see Exs. 10(vi) and 11(v)).

· There are biological psychiatrists who attempt to solve all problems by massive pharmacotherapy. Feelings of inadequacy, difficulties in family relations, being rejected and perhaps inviting rejection are ignored or expected to go away.

> Ex. 11(vi). Peter, 35, had been in our group for a number of years. He was an intelligent man and grammar school educated. He had been married and was divorced, apparently because of violent behaviour. Of his many brothers, one had been hospitalized, diagnosed schizophrenic. Peter himself had been so diagnosed, though there seemed to be no basis for this. 'I wish I **were** crazy,' he would say. He suffered from obsessive ruminations, and was also unable to bear deferment of his wishes: what he wanted, he wanted now. This contributed to his aggressiveness, mostly verbal but at times physical. He spoke much of feeling rejected; more than once he expressed admiration for people who had committed suicide 'so as not to be a burden on the family.'

The group did its best to help Peter, often becoming exasperated and requiring the conductors' support and mediation. We also received the father in the group once monthly, to deal with his many requests to talk to the therapists.

Peter lived alone; his family hosted him alternate weekends. (The group had much to say on this relative inhospitality.) One day Peter asked the hospital to take him in over the weekend, as he could not face a weekend alone.

At first the hospital doctors were reluctant to admit him: how could he be ill when he himself requested admission?

They did admit him, and began to change his medication, a reasonable use of the admission. A powerful antipsychotic was given, together with valium. Discussing this with his ward doctor I ventured that valium was unlikely to calm him. As to the powerful antipsychotic, he was not psychotic. 'Yes, but I had one case of obsessional ruminations who was helped by it.' Peter had asked if he might continue to come to the group, as in past admissions. He was refused. We, the co-therapists, missed him, so did the group. It felt like losing a child, a problem child, but still ours.

After three months he was at last released and attended the absorption group of the clinic. Then he disappeared. I called his parents. 'Peter is back in hospital; he is very ill,' his mother told me. 'He has been put on a new drug. He does not speak at all. He does not even ask to come home; he asks for nothing. This is not the Peter I know.' The drug was Clozapine.

This is an example of endeavouring to solve all problems by pharmacotherapy, authoritarianism and shutting the patient away from the family.

Pullen (1999, p.381) writes of his use of medication in a young adults' unit: 'Medication is only used to attempt to help with symptoms to the extent that the patient finds them distressing, or of course, to reduce any risks posed to the lives of the patients or to others. It is not the staff's role to eliminate "delusions".' This sums the issue up well.

In summary, the therapeutic community for psychotic patients need not necessarily abjure the benefits of pharmacotherapy, used in moderation. It would, however, regard psychological approaches as most important.

The therapeutic community and the long-stay patient

Do we need a therapeutic community for long-stay patients? What is wrong with a well-functioning modern hospital, with open doors and facilities for occupational therapy?

Let me begin with another example.

Ex. 11(vii). At one time I worked half-time on D ward, a long-stay ward with open doors. It seemed pleasant enough, though I noticed that the 'motherly' ward sister had patients line up for soap and towel when they wanted a shower. They had to ask for single cigarettes, and were also given a cigarette in recompense for little chores. (This did not prevent them from continuous smoking.)

There were twice weekly group meetings, led by a social worker and myself, dating back from before my time. However, they were dull. Much time was given to complaints about food, and little of importance was said. The countertransference feelings were depression, impotence, emptiness.

I invited the ward sister for a meeting with all the nurses from both shifts. She proclaimed it a good idea. When the time came, she had 'forgotten'. The same happened with another attempt. Clearly, I could not change the atmosphere of the groups without working with the nurses to change the climate of the ward, and there was no openness to this.

In this connection I want to talk about Mark. He was about 50, not psychotic, not depressed, and in no way acutely disturbed. However, when I tried to get to know him, he had very little to say. He had little to say about his life history. More strikingly, he had no hopes or plans for the future. I could not interest him in anything. I went to London for postgraduate training for a year, and on my return was assigned to the Internal Rehabilitation Unit (IRU), which was a therapeutic community, part of the hospital yet independently run by social workers, occupational therapists and psychologists. (There were no nurses.) I was to be the psychiatrist.

Here I met Mark again. He was now in charge of the household, together with a woman resident. This involved ordering food from the main kitchen, serving and sometimes cooking it, ordering household supplies, organizing the washing up. Mark was a different person. He was happy, confident and very good at this job.

There was a monthly residents' meeting in the evening, in which residents were free to bring up any problem they wished. Mark was very active in managing this meeting, though the staff still kept formal charge. I suggested to the staff team that we hand this meeting entirely to the residents to manage, and have them elect a chairman. They elected Mark, who collected items for the agenda and chaired the meeting very efficiently.

A special project on a conventional ward

A special rehabilitation project on D ward had been disappointing. A senior psychologist had been engaged to rehabilitate a selected group of 24 patients; he was given auxiliary staff. At the end of a year, only one patient was able to work outside the hospital. I think the main reason for the limited success is that patients were not given genuine responsibility. Neither were they expected to help one another. The expert care they received was a 'gift' from the staff.

Countertransference in work with chronic schizophrenics

As I described, conducting a group of chronic schizophrenics on D ward produced in me a sense of getting nowhere, despondency, depression. It was very different from the countertransference feeling with other kinds of groups, including groups with acute psychotic patients. I found that colleagues were often reluctant to take such groups.

Lefevre (1994, pp.441–447) has analysed the countertransference feelings of nurses facilitating groups with chronic psychotic patients in a large London hospital: in the first phase, there was emptiness and bewilderment, later there was frustration, then sadness and feeling drained, then anxiety, finally reality testing, wondering if they were good enough, or having a sense of achievement. Many nurse facilitators became physically ill.

Lefevre saw a need for special training. In a later paper Lefevre (1999) describes the evolution of a successful rehabilitation project which included systematic psychodynamic training for nurses. She points to early difficulties: her problems in persuading senior clinicians of the need for the project, and of making sense of the projections received by nurses in the course of their daily work, including aggression. Those who doubt are referred to the work of Searles (1965), who describes various feelings experienced in therapy with such patients, including murderous ones. She herself quotes him as emphasising the importance of the therapist regressing in the therapeutic process in order to experience and hold on to the patient's pain and madness, not to go mad but to be with the madness. In this project, the nurses learnt to tolerate these feelings, to act as containers to the patients' projections and to understand the patients' own feelings of guilt and despair.

My own experience shows that difficult countertransference feelings arise more often in groups with chronic psychotic patients than with acute ones, and that the therapeutic community orientation diminishes such difficulties (for example, in work in the Internal Rehabilitation Unit, described in this chapter).

Responsibility, effectiveness and meaning

We all look for meaning in life. Mentally ill persons are no exception. They can possibly bear to be dependent on others for a brief period of acute illness, but beyond that, a life without aim or direction is debilitating and depressing.

It is taken for granted that adults carry responsibility in life, not only for themselves, but also for other persons and things: their children, other members of their family; their household and usually also an area in their field of work. Chronic mental patients tend to be bereft of responsibility and therefore infantilized. (We have seen some examples of this infantilization on the ward on which I worked: a patient could not even have a shower on his own, or take a cigarette out of his own packet. To be responsible for someone or something other than himself was out of the question.)

Clark (1974) wrote:

> The big organization tends to take away an individual's responsibility and make him passive, hostile and dependent. Doctors and nurses are highly skilled at removing an individual's responsibility. This is necessary for a person who is physically ill and in high fever; he needs to regress into dependence. But it is very crippling over the months and years – and often quite unnecessary.

Clark is quoted by Pullen (1999, pp.363–364), who continues: 'Allowing patients "responsibility" was, and is, the real challenge that continues to be resisted by professionals.'

I suggest that one of the main therapeutic factors in the therapeutic community for psychotic patients is the sharing and assigning of responsibility. This restores self-respect and gives life a sense of purpose and meaning. When they have a responsible task in the community, this gives them a feeling of being needed. They have to function in the real world, even if they still have some psychotic fantasies.

When patients have responsibility in the community, they take the group meeting seriously. They know they are expected to help one another, and this is also made clear in the method of conducting the group. When they find that they can be effective in helping another group member, this gives an additional boost to their self-esteem.

Patients who have been regarded as 'chronic' may thus change in the therapeutic community. I believe that chronicity is not so much a function of the 'illness' as a defence against the emptiness of life in hospital, against meaninglessness.

Every person needs to be needed

Barham (1998) finds that the personhood of the mental patient is generally neglected. He writes: 'their potential as human beings capable of giving as much as receiving was generally disregarded'. He emphasizes 'the importance of being able to make a difference to something, affect something' (Barham 1998, pp.222, 223).

Clark, a pioneer of the therapeutic community approach, writes: 'It was several years before I even began to consider the possibility that patients could actually help each other – or that there might be patients who could help each other better than the doctors did' (Barham 1998, p.225).

The internal rehabilitation unit

The Internal Rehabilitation Unit, which defined itself as a therapeutic community, had been in existence for about a year when I was assigned to it. It was part of a conventional hospital but had a certain amount of autonomy. The staff were social workers, psychologists and occupational therapists. There were no nurses, which was probably a significant factor in autonomy; patients went to one of the wards to take their medication. A social worker and occupational therapist were defined as being in charge, while I was to be the unit psychiatrist. There were 24 residents, men and women, of various ages; all had been in hospital for some time.

On my arrival, this was the structure: residents were divided into four small groups of six, each with two therapists, who met with them once a week and had responsibilities for them. There was a 'large group' meeting of half an hour each morning, from which inside as well as outside workers were excused. There was a residents' meeting one evening a month, in which administrative decisions were made. Staff roles were not differentiated. As to domestic arrangements, the unit was run by the 'catering group', two residents helped by one staff member. They were responsible for the catering, involving ordering food and raw materials from the main hospital, in some cases cooking it, always organizing the serving of it and the washing up. Residents not otherwise employed had to be in an activity group, which meant either gardening or cooking: the cooking group made soup which was consumed at lunch.

I was at once faced with a choice in the nature of my role as psychiatrist. I was asked, in fact, if I wanted to be involved in the community or be aloof. I could, thus, have sat in an office and acted like a medical consultant, perhaps exercised some authority. This, however, would have limited my role and left me outside the life of the therapeutic community. I opted, unhesitatingly, for being fully involved. I would be in a patients' work group, and sit down at table with them. As to making changes, I would have to work on these with the team, and with the residents.

Staff anxieties

It turned out that residents tended to have more ideas for and be more open to change than the staff. Martin (1962) points to an initial increase in anxiety when changes towards a therapeutic community are first made. In my experience, staff anxieties were much more prominent.

One example concerned the residents' budget. Should staff help them in managing it, or should they be left to flounder and learn from experience? The latter meant disappointment, perhaps frustration for the resident, but was more educative in the long run. It took time, however, for most of the staff to become convinced.

Another example was the case of Tirza and Alex, two residents who had fallen in love. Alex had been buying presents for Tirza. The staff spoke of Tirza's demandingness, of her 'exploiting' Alex. They expressed a fear that Tirza, the more sick of the two, would pull Alex down. Should they intervene?

Within two months, staff attitudes changed. No one spoke of intervening any longer. It had become clear that Alex and Tirza had both benefited from the relationship. Alex, from being glum and introspective, had become more alert and more sociable. Tirza, who had always complained of weakness and inability to work, was now doing her washing up duty and taking part in work groups. Alex asked to return to his job in a sheltered workshop in town which he had left some years earlier. He had some initial difficulty but he persevered.

The idea of the loan fund

A member of the newly elected residents' committee thought up a scheme for organizing small loans. The accepted procedure was to put this to the residents' meeting. Being controversial, the liaison staff member brought the issue to the staff meeting. Some staff thought that the scheme would encourage reckless spending and should be quashed. The liaison staff member (myself) argued that any idea of a resident deserved to be taken seriously and should be put to the vote at the residents' meeting. After discussion in several meetings, staff agreed to bring the scheme to the residents' meeting. The vote was in favour and it was put into operation.

The paradox of permissiveness

Contrary to what is usually believed, permissiveness does not mean a paucity of rules. Rules which are explicit and clearly defined make life easier rather than more difficult. In the absence of a washing up rota, it may turn out that no one washes up, or that the same people take it on themselves every time. Residents may be accused of not volunteering, of not pulling their weight. The rota organizes things and makes them easier.

Neither is flexibility in enforcing rules a good thing. If staff decide that residents ought to sign a book on going to town, this has to be enforced. If resident A. is not held to account for not letting staff know, but B. is, because he causes concern, or for whatever reason, the system becomes paternalistic.

The best and best-kept rules are those made by the residents themselves. This is what happened with the morning meeting.

The case of the morning meeting

When I joined the unit, the morning meeting was, as I mentioned, not compulsory. Not only outside workers, but also those who worked in the hospital, were excused. This led to others taking advantage of this laxity; attendance was poor. I found that the meeting was too poorly attended to discuss unit business, and too short for dynamics to develop. It was a mere formality.

One day Gideon expressed anger that so many residents were absent. His roommates had not been pulling their weight in cleaning the room, but he could not effectively discuss this in their absence. The group discussed the matter of attendance and decided that it should be compulsory. An attendance register was started at that point. At the residents' meeting that month, residents decided that whoever did not attend the morning meeting five times running had no place in the unit. From that point, attendance improved remarkably; it rose from around 40 per cent to around 80 per cent (the absentees included those who worked in town).

I believe the effectiveness of the rule was due to its having been formulated by the residents. It now made sense to extend the time of the meeting to an hour. It had effectively become a large group.

Large and small groups

My impression had been that the small groups of six were too small to have a group character. Absence of one group member made this worse. Because of the number of residents (twenty-four) and of staff (eight) it was difficult to change this. Fortunately, the daily large group was becoming more meaningful and more therapeutic.

The importance of bringing issues to the large group

Should therapists respond individually to residents' specific, possibly trivial requests? Some might think it a good idea. Yet there is much to be said for referring them to the large group.

One morning, at breakfast, Hannah approached me and asked me to prescribe sleeping tablets. I asked her to bring this up in the morning group. This she did. She was asked why she could not sleep. It turned out that she had been troubled by seeing Rose go to Alex's room. Alex had a steady girlfriend, Tirza, as was known to everyone in the unit. The group, including those concerned, expressed their feelings on the matter. Clearly, this was important and what Hannah had wanted was to bring up and discuss this matter in front of all concerned. The sleeping pill was merely an admission ticket.

Rehabilitation outside the hospital

Because of the failure of the intensive rehabilitation scheme on D ward (mentioned in this chapter), it was believed that patients of this degree of chronicity could not be rehabilitated outside hospital. Yet many residents asked to go home, claiming rightly that they worked, their health was stable, and there was no reason to keep them. My own positioning tending to go along with this was considered rather heretical.

Arguments were that residents would have difficulty outside and would be discouraged. Moreover, most of their families were not overjoyed at the thought of having them back. The expected setbacks would make them more ill; it was thus preferable to discourage them from leaving. My argument was that residents should be allowed to make their own mistakes and learn from them; I was almost alone in this view.

Later, staff attitudes changed. A plan was made to rehabilitate the first four residents in a town flat. A staff member would visit and be on call for support. They would join therapy groups in the outpatient clinic. This worked very well. Of the original group of four leavers, only one returned to hospital. A social worker with initiative, Rachel Beenstock, later founded an 'external rehabilitation unit' and rehabilitated groups of patients in hostels she established in town, with a therapeutic community character.

Conclusion

Every therapeutic community is different; there is no one right way of running one. Characteristics will to some extent depend on the nature of the environment, as well as the personality of the therapists and their willingness to respect the patient, as well as undergo change themselves, to involve themselves as persons rather than someone playing a professional role. This is a learning process; as we find in accounts of students and staff in the Arbours Communities (Berke *et al.* 1995), therapists have to be able to accept the residents' projections, thus becoming emotionally vulnerable yet retain the ability to think.

When I worked in Napsbury Hospital, near St Albans, in the 1960s, there was a hostel ward. There was a 'bureau' which found jobs for patients outside the hospital, and an agency which found landladies willing to give them a home on leaving the hospital. It worked. It did not call itself a therapeutic community, but those who devised the system clearly believed in the potential of the patient.

Chronicity, and the passivity, dependence and chronic hopelessness that go with it, are a product of the environment, not a result of disease. Most chronic schizophrenics and others can be rehabilitated.

The acutely ill, experiencing the trauma of first breakdown, need not suffer the additional insult of being segregated, locked up and treated as a patient with a disease rather than a person in distress. They can be helped to make sense of their crisis or their illness, and to integrate it into their lives. In this, too, the therapeutic community approach is very important.

CHAPTER 12

The Couples Group

Foulkes (1975, p.23) writes of couples groups, which he classifies under 'groups formed in view of their common problem'. Though his personal experience of such groups was not extensive, he took an interest in them. He was not surprised when a therapist of a group of parents of schizophrenic children found neurotic problems in the parents. Foulkes regarded it as important that the couples composing a group did not meet outside the session, just like individual members of a group, and that they were committed to preserve their marriage. He called the couples group 'a hybrid of a group analytic group and a family group.'

The couples group is, like the multiple family therapy group, a compound group, a group composed of groups. It is a three-dimensional system (see Chapter 2).

Consider the dimensions of the couples group. Zero Dimension is the intrapsychic. Dimension One is intra-couple. Dimension Two is intra-group, where there are many possibilities: between couples, between individuals, between an individual and the group, between a couple and the group, between men and women. Dimension Three is between group and therapist.

Zero Dimension	Intrapsychic
Dimension One	Intra-couple
Dimension Two	Intra-group. Interaction between couples, between one couple and the group, between one individual and the group
Dimension Three	Between group and therapist(s)

Figure 12.1 Dimensions of the couples group.

My personal involvement with couples groups began with a workshop by James Framo. He gave me a feeling of confidence about such groups, although I did not, in fact, stick to his rather structured method. Here I want to pay tribute to my late co-therapist, Immanuel Cohen, who volunteered to take the first couples group with me, and the second. He had had experience with a couples group in the Israel Defence Forces; it was a group for men with traumatic neuroses and their wives. Our first group was a very open one, the policy being to admit every couple in the clinic who needed help. The problem could be either with their relationship or with one of their children. This was interesting, but uneven and problematic because of lack of commitment.

Our next project was a closed group for three couples. When one couple dropped out, we replaced them. We also added a fourth couple who dropped out after a time. When I went to London for a year, we decided that the group ought not to continue with just one therapist. On my return, I found that they had been meeting in one another's houses, once weekly, during the whole year. It was a continuous 'alternative group'. I was requested to continue as their therapist on my return. Dr Cohen, to my regret, was unable to return to co-therapy of the group because of health problems. Sadly, he died after an open heart operation some time later. He had been a perfect co-therapist, balancing my way of intervening with his own. In the after-group discussions, he had a unique way of encouraging me in the development of my ideas, seamlessly completing them with some of his own. Thus we evolved some concepts about the working of the group. I wrote a paper about the group under both our names; we did not succeed in publishing it at the time. This chapter will, I hope, make up for this to some extent.

After terminating the second group, I ran a third cycle of couples group with Moshe Krupnik, a social worker at the clinic. Because of the fragility of a three-couples group I had decided that five couples would make a better basis. Then, if a couple was absent for any reason, there would still be a group. Krupnik was in favour of setting a time limit and we decided that two years would be a suitable period. A year later, and two years later, we invited the group for a follow-up meeting. Altogether, I had been conducting couples groups for ten years.

Selection for couples groups

The main criterion for acceptance in the couples group is the willingness to commit oneself, which is of obvious importance. When one person in a group of individuals is absent or drops out, there is still a group. When one couple in a group of three couples drops out, there is no group. We found it quite difficult to get sufficient couples to make a group, even in a busy outpatient clinic with some awareness of the importance of work with family systems. Couples tend to be more reluctant than individuals to join a group. I kept couples on the waiting list by recurrently meeting with them, to prepare them for the group and to ensure they would not drop out.

There are three kinds of indications for joining a couples group:

- conflict between the partners
- neurotic problems in one (or both) partners
- problems with one or more of the children.

The second and third categories may need comment. Why include both partners, when 'pathology' is apparently lodged in one of them? When one partner has a neurotic problem, it tends to be perpetuated by the 'healthy' partner, who has become accustomed to his or her role as the 'strong' one. I quoted Rycroft (1966, p.11) in Chapter 1: 'Symptoms are not entirely an individual matter – they have a social nexus and function and change in one person may be contingent on changes in others.' Although Rycroft did not specifically practise family therapy, and wrote this before it became widespread, he emphasized the role of the spouse in perpetuating (or otherwise) of the symptom.

> For instance, if a married man is impotent or sexually perverted his recovery depends not only on his understanding of the origins of his disability, but also on whether his wife really and truly welcomes his recovery, and on whether, if she doesn't, he feels prepared to overcome her reluctance, or, if that seems impossible, to make alternative arrangements. (Rycroft 1966, pp.10–11)

To give an example from our group, one woman developed severe agoraphobia. It turned out that before its development there had been a good deal of marital conflict. After she developed the phobia, conflict was no longer in evidence. The husband, who had to protect her and accompany her when she went out, seemed to enjoy his new role. Possibly, the wife did too. She had, however, given up her work as a nurse.

As to problems with children, I refer the reader back to Chapter 1 to Lily Pincus's little girl who climbed trees (Ex. 1(i)). Since two years of therapy with the child had made no impression, the couple were taken into therapy. They revealed themselves as extremely cautious, never taking the slightest risk. For example, when told that another pregnancy would endanger the wife's health, they decided that abstinence was the only safe way of ensuring this would not happen. It became clear that the risk-taking had been projected into their little daughter.

In our most recent group, two of the five couples were concerned only about their children. One complained about behaviour and learning difficulties of their 12-year-old son. The father proclaimed that he himself was not in need of treatment but would come to please his wife. We found that the couple had much to work on. In the second case, a middle son was in therapy (with another psycho-therapist) for immaturity and identity diffusion; he had not been accepted for service in the Israel Defence Forces (IDF), which, in Israel, is a social stigma. We found some clearly Oedipal features in family relationships: for example, the parents' bedroom had no door at all. The first concrete achievement of the preparatory sessions was the installation of a door. On termination of his personal therapy, and the termination of our group, the young man was accepted by the IDF.

There are distinct advantages in mixing diagnostic categories in this way. Where there was a group of couples with parenting problems, they would be tempted to discuss just those, thereby reinforcing their anxieties over their children. When diagnoses are mixed, there is a good chance the focus will be on the dynamics of the whole family, which are important whatever the diagnoses. We also know that when members of a group all have similar defences, they reinforce each other; mixing different diagnostic categories increases the chance of couples having different defences. Another advantage is that some group members will be strong in one area, and able to help others who are weak in that area, and vice versa.

The group process

Just as group members help one another in the group of individuals, couples in the couples group help one another, individuals help couples, couples help individuals, and the group as a whole makes its contribution. The therapist's primary task is to facilitate these processes.

To get a better idea of the group process, let us look at a map of dimensions in the couples group (Figure 12.2). This will give us an idea not only of interactions, but also of the perspectives at each level.

Figure 12.2 gives a idea of the rich possibilities, but it is not exhaustive. For example, in the intra-group space, one couple can have a perspective on the interaction in another couple. A couple can have a perspective on an individual, or an individual on a couple (or, of course, an individual on another individual). A couple can have a metaperspective on how a couple sees itself. The group as a whole can have a perspective on the interaction in a couple, or on the role of an individual in a group. Thus, in the case of someone who had become very aggressive towards the therapists, the group observed this and pointed it out. Less easily, the group can have a perspective on itself, or an individual can have a perspective on the group.

As to the therapist or therapist pair, in Figure 12.2 I have given perspectives specific to them. Of course, the therapist has a perspective on an individual (and his intrapsychic world), but this is not the main focus here. The therapist also has a perspective on what happens between partners; this is something shared with the group.

Dimension	Interaction	Perspective
0	Intrapsychic	Wife on herself WW Husband on himself HH
1	Intra-couple	Each partner's view of the other metaperspectives; how H thinks W sees herself, etc. Meta-metaperspectives: how W thinks H thinks she sees herself, and vice versa
2	Intra-group e.g. between couples, between individual and a couple, between men and women, etc.	Group on couple Group on an individual Individual on a couple Couple on another Couple on an individual Group on itself, etc.
3	Between group and therapist(s)	Group on therapist(s), incl. T Therapist(s) on groups and individuals (T interpretations) Metaperspectives: therapist's view of group on a couple, etc.

Figure 12.2 Dimensions and perspectives of the couples group.

The therapist could make interpretations on the interaction between partners, could conduct single couple therapy in the group. This has drawbacks. He is easily perceived as prejudiced in favour of one or other partner. In the case of one couple in our group, the husband had once been in individual therapy with me. I had occasionally seen them together as a couple. The wife was convinced that I was prejudiced against her. On the other hand, when the group made observations about the couple's mode of relating, this was acceptable to both partners. The group was not perceived as prejudiced, hence their intervention was more effective.

The therapist has a wide choice of possible interventions in the couples group. He could intervene in Dimension One, interacting with an individual. Alternatively, he could work in Dimension Two, making observations on a couple. However, to do either of these is to fail to make use of the group process. The group itself has a perspective on and is capable of treating a couple (as in the above example), and can often do it more effectively.

The therapists can share their metaperspective and comment, if necessary, on the group's observations on a couple: they may emphasize, amplify or correct these if indicated. They may want to comment on what happens in the group as a whole. As in all groups, they are also required to intervene in the group process when it gets stuck or goes wrong.

To sum up, there are a number of reasons for being sparing with interventions in Dimensions One and Two:

- They foster dependence on the therapist, who comes to be perceived as the only helper.

- Through them, the therapist may be seduced into individual therapy in the group, which is an endless task.

- When the focus is on the individual rather than the system, it conveys that the 'identified patient' is 'sick' and the partner is 'healthy'. The aim of the group is, however, to involve the healthy or stronger spouse in change.

- When the therapists intervene in Dimensions One and Two, they inhibit the group process. They compete with the group in functions it can fulfil. Robin Skynner (1976) suggests, waiting to allow others to interpret or act instead, as they usually do if the therapist gives them space.

A theory of conflict in couples

An important factor in bringing about conflict between partners is the difference in perception of self and other, and of their respective roles. As Laing *et al.* (1966) showed, such differences may lead, without any bad intention, to arguments which escalate into conflict. One partner may assume that there will be mutual give-and-take, whereas the other may expect submission to his authority.

We recall the example of Anthony and Sarah (Ex. 1(vi)), who told the therapist they had quarrelled and could not understand what started it. Anthony had suggested going to a film. He had made a special effort, he related, because she had often disliked his choice of films in the past. He therefore wanted to make sure that this time she would really approve of his choice. As he told it, she became very angry when he asked her and refused to come.

Sarah's version was this: Anthony asked her to come to a specific film, and repeatedly asked her if she really wanted to go. From this she understood that he did not really want to take her. As she put it to the children, he was making fun of her. Hence she refused to go.

When both partners related their version, it became clear to the couple that there had been no bad intentions. This took place in therapy with the couple alone.

In the group, it is likely that other couples, or other individuals, will see the issue brought up by a couple in a different light. Rather than being stuck in a black–white, wrong–right conundrum, the couple will come to see that there is a spectrum of colours. Each will be enabled to see that their perspective is only one of many possible ones.

The dynamics between partners: Bateson's theory of schismogenesis

Bateson (1972[1935]) analysed possible relationships between cultural groups in anthropology (Culture contact and schismogenesis, 1935). They also apply to couples. There may be symmetrical differentiation, complementary differentiation, or reciprocity. The first two lead to an escalating spiral, or schismogenesis. The last is balanced.

In symmetrical differentiating, each partner reacts with the same behaviour: for example, trying to prove themselves right. They thus compete, each fighting for ascendancy, with conflict escalating in a vicious spiral which Bateson calls schismogenesis.

In complementary differentiation, one partner is dependent, while the other is dominant. The dependence of the one makes the other more dominant, and vice versa: the dependent one becomes more and more afraid of the dominant partner, and takes less and less initiative. The dominant one feels he or she must grasp the reins even more firmly, and so on. In this case too there is schismogenesis.

In reciprocity, partner A. will help partner B. in one area, while B. will help A. in another. They agree that A. will be responsible for finances, while B. will be in charge of the children's education. The relationship is balanced.

The therapeutic task in schismogenesis

Couples with a dominant–dependent configuration frequently come to therapy and are not easy to treat. It is not enough to treat the weak, dependent partner, though he or she will be the 'designated patient'. The strong partner has to change too. On the whole, it is easier to involve both partners in change in the group, as opposed to single couple therapy.

Defences and difficulties in the couples group

Collusion and avoidance

One problem that arises, in particular with closed groups, is that they learn to avoid sensitive issues. They learn, unconsciously, not to step on one another's toes. I noticed this particularly with the group which had been meeting on their own for a year. When I returned to work with them, at their request, I found them too comfortable, too much lacking in anxiety or motivation to change. The problem might still be there, but it was extremely difficult to move anything.

Taking the role of therapist

A woman in one of the groups frequently made psychological observations. In fact, she took on the role of group psychologist, which enabled her to avoid bringing herself as patient. On one occasion, she was asked to talk about herself. Her response was to describe her problems with her husband, thus bringing him as patient instead.

Late in the group, she recalled her relationship with her mother in childhood. I deliberately ignored the transference aspect of this, as I thought it important to encourage her to talk about herself and her childhood.

Controlling group members

Just as a manic patient can destroy a group of individuals, a dominant and control-ling member can destroy a couples group. It seems that such a person's controlling tendencies are channelled into the marital relationship while avoiding being diagnosed as a unipolar illness or even hypomanic disorder. In one group we had a woman who dominated her husband and the group. She conducted marital dis-cussions by reiterating her own point, refusing to hear her husband, and preventing him from speaking by raising her own voice. The therapists were in a dilemma about asking her to leave, until she dropped out on her own initiative. In such a case, it may be questioned whether the remaining partner should be allowed to stay in the group. In this case we decided that he should.

Strong hate

There were two couples in which one spouse (in each case the wife) turned out to be full of hate for the other. The fact that both partners willingly entered therapy may blind one to this fact. One may argue that in such cases it is better for the couple to separate, but in both cases the 'weak' partner expressed no interest in this.

The power of the group

From clinical observation, we can identify some of the processes which appear to be therapeutic.

The group provides an additional perspective

As described above, partners may perceive themselves differently from the way they are perceived by the other, and this can lead to conflict which may escalate. The group is in a particularly good position to demonstrate to couples that there is more than one way of perceiving the other. The partners come to see their perception is only one of many possible ones.

> Ex. 12(i). Consider a couple, Pam and Stanley. Pam asks for her accustomed attention, since she regards herself as an overworked mother. Stanley regards her as demanding and does nothing. Pam sees him as unhelpful and reiterates her request. Stanley becomes irritated and they both become progressively more angry.
>
> We might say that the conflicted couple are 'locked' in their perceptions of self and other. Each feels that theirs is the 'true' view. When they bring their problem to the group, other group members contribute their views. Gradually, this shows the spouses the relativity of their perceptions.
>
> In our example, Pamela has seen herself as the overworked mother badly in need of help, while Stanley saw her as a 'sergeant-major'. One man in the group pointed out that Stanley must have been tired after returning from work. One woman asked Pam how she phrased her demands. (This couple's relationship was much improved through the group.)

At times a group member is drawn into 'judging' the couple, pronouncing who is right. The therapists can then point out what is happening.

We can present the perceptions of a couple schematically (Figure 12.3) (see also Chapter 6).

WW	wife's view of herself
H(WW)	how husband thinks wife sees herself
H(WH)	how husband thinks wife sees him

Also

HH	husband's view of himself
W(HH)	how wife thinks husband sees himself
W(HW)	how wife thinks husband sees her

Figure 12.3 Spouses' perceptions and metaperceptions.

A group member perceives wife in a specific way: M1(H) and has a view of how wife perceives husband – M1(WH)

Another group member has a view of how husband sees wife – M2(HW). We could go on to meta-metaperceptions, but shall stop here for simplicity.

The members thus gain additional perspectives of the group on each of them, and on their relationship as a couple. This enables them to see beyond their original narrow view of one another.

Partners learn by projective identification

Yalom (1981) writes of 'vicarious learning', which he defines as learning by observing the therapy of others in the group. This is a conscious process; beyond this, I find that a group member can learn through a process involving projection. She may perceive a character trait or a problem in another which corresponds to a similar trait or problem in herself. She may originally be unaware of the trait in herself, but the process of seeing it in others may enable her to look at herself.

This appears to be related to 'negative mirroring', which Pines (1998) describes thus:

> something that we dislike in the other person will represent hidden and unwanted aspects of ourselves. Time and again this turns out to be true in the group: that what we are not turns out in the end to be what we are. So long as these differences are negotiable, then progress can be made towards the under-standing and integration of these rejected and unwanted aspects of the self. (Pines 1998, p.33)

We saw clear examples of learning through projection in the couples group.

> Ex. 12(ii). Sheila Green talks about her phobic fears of going out. She feels no improvement. When she makes efforts to overcome them, she ends up with a violent headache. Norman White remarks: 'I think I know your problem. You are trying to be what you once were.'

Sheila is amazed and pleased; he has hit the nail on the head. The therapist, and then the group, encourage her to enlarge on this. She tells them that when she 'overcomes' her phobia she has to do it in a big way – not only cook the supper but also make a cake. When friends come she has to serve a large number of dishes.

Wanting to be what he once was is Norman's own problem. Like Sheila, he is a perfectionist. What he wants is to be the successful executive he was 'before the illness'. He has sensitively perceived the problem in Sheila, when it was not at all evident. To whatever extent he is aware of it in himself, he is not yet able to face up to it.

> Ex. 12(iii). The group was talking about children. Debbie Black complained that her husband took her from them almost violently when he wanted her for himself. Edna White asked why he had to do this; she must be too closely involved with the children. Debbie replied: 'He has been jealous since they were born.' Edna wondered about Debbie's sex life; Debbie replied that it was fine. 'But one's relationship with a man is not confined to the bedroom,' retorted

Debbie. It is no coincidence that Edna can see this problem in Debbie's marriage; she herself sees herself as the expert parent, the expert educator of their three children. Her husband can hardly get a look in.

It appears that by working with his own problem as it appears in another person, the group member deals with his own conflict at an acceptable distance. In time, he is able to work through it directly in himself, overtly or quietly.

The group involves the strong partner in the need for change

As already mentioned, the partner with neurotic problems cannot change unless the 'strong' one does so too. Bowen (1976) holds that therapy is most effective if the strong partner can be induced to change. Yet the single couple therapist may find it difficult to effect such change. The 'strong' partner feels fine: having well-integrated defences. The 'strong' partner may receive some gratification from the adopted role (though the 'weak' one may do so too).

The group has more power to involve both partners in change. It provides a non-judgemental atmosphere which facilitates the expression of feelings in both partners.

Ex. 12(iv). Gideon Black opens the meeting. 'Take your coat off,' he says to Jack Green, 'today I am going to go for you. Why do you never talk in the group?' Green replies that he did not want his wife to get angry. She is easily upset. He himself tries to remain cool. He never cries.

Jack tells the group that his wife and he fight over the most trivial things. He gives an example: his wife wanted put-away beds for their little boys. He thought bunk beds would make more sense; they took up less space and made less work. It was only logical.

Sheila Green explains that she hates bunk beds. Jack repeats that she is not being logical. Norman White intervenes: logic does not come into it. 'On the other hand,' says Gideon, 'he means it for her good.' One of the therapists points out that Gideon has done good work so far. However, it is not a matter of judging between the partners. The point is not who is right, but it is important that each should try to see the other's point of view.

The argument about the beds is now discontinued. Sheila moves to what turns out to be a deeper level of their conflict. 'My husband punishes me by not doing repairs.' Gideon Black suggests she might be punishing him; men are tired on coming home from work. Edna White asks what he punishes her for. Sheila replies: 'All sorts of things…neglecting him…not giving him sex. He says I am not his.'

This opens up an area of grievance not previously disclosed to the group. Sheila explains: if she gives herself to him, she is treated like a queen; if not, she is punished in all kinds of subtle ways. Jack Green explains: he does everything for his wife, he is a good provider, he helps her in the house, he looks after her when she is sick. Gideon Black suggests he is 'buying' her. Edna White is aghast: this is sex under compulsion. Had she been in Sheila's shoes, she would have killed herself long ago. Gideon sympathizes with Jack: one comes home tense, one needs sex to unwind. His wife says: 'What are we coming to? Sex to get rid of tension? Are we animals?'

Jack says his wife sometimes talks of sex as something animal-like. Perhaps she is frigid. Sheila replies that she sometimes wonders if she is normal. But she is a woman, she is interested. It is the pressure that spoils it all. Norman makes an interpretation: 'Jack, you use sex in place of everything. You don't cry. You don't relax. You don't show feelings.'

We note that therapist intervention has been minimal, the group itself has been a very good therapist. Jack Green accepted it with a good grace, responding to its searching questions about himself and beginning to abandon his rigid defences. When he had been in single couple therapy, he had stubbornly maintained his stance as the 'strong one' who has no need to get involved.

The group provides a field for trying new forms of relating

This is the case in every group, but is particularly important in the couples group. Each partner in a couple is accustomed to a specific role in the marriage. Thus, the husband of a dominating and critical wife has become fearful, lacking in initiative, trying to please his wife all the time. His wife urges him to be more assertive and take more initiative, but this is of course a paradoxical injunction.

In the group, however, he can play a different role. The group shows appreciation of various qualities of his, perhaps for the first time. He can help other couples and exercise his strong points. He can take new initiatives without fear of being criticized. Conversely, consider a dominant husband whose wife is afraid of him (like Jack, in our last example). In the group, his actions and their meanings are for the first time submitted to scrutiny. His 'manly' qualities of never crying, never showing any feelings are exposed as not showing strength at all, but as a defence against experiencing emotions.

The couples group has greater stability than the couple–therapist system

The therapist working with a single couple is easily drawn into an alliance with one or other partner. In my personal experience, countertransference might make me side with the 'weak' partner against the 'strong', in an apparent attempt to right the balance. In one case the 'weak' partner complained bitterly about my partiality.

Co-therapy can help to counteract this tendency. The Milan method, based on making hypotheses involving the whole family system (or the couple as a whole) also avoids such bias; consultation with the professional team consolidates neutrality.

A couple can 'manipulate' a therapist into a specific position. When a depressed woman in her fifties, a Holocaust survivor, moved to Jerusalem, I decided that I would treat the spouses together. Marital problems were indeed prominent. Yet I found myself increasingly irritated by the wife's verbosity and habit of interrupting the other. At the end of a workshop by the Sharffs, at question time, I decided to bring the couple as a problem. It was uncomfortable to admit difficulty to a large audience of fellow-professionals. However, the suggestions from colleagues helped me gain perspective, and I was able to see the wife's suffering more sympathetically. This was useful in the subsequent course of therapy.

Of course, a supervision group would be helpful in a similar way.

In the couples group, group members, by the nature of things, perceive the partners and the couple as a whole in different ways (provided they are allowed to do their work in Dimension One). This tends to prevent the sort of countertransference distortion that occurs in single couple therapy.

The diachronic process

I have said much about the synchronic group process. As to the diachronic process, it must be said that not every couple is helped. There were some drop-outs. Two couples were not helped; in these there was massive hate on the part of at least one partner (in each case, the wife). Psychotherapy can do many things, but turning hate into love or even respect is extremely difficult.

In general, stages could be discerned in the group:

1. Consolidation of the group

2. Conflict work

3. Individuation

4. Return to conflict work and work on the relationship.

In the case of couples where one partner had symptoms, it took longer to get to the stage of conflict work.

CHAPTER 13

The Median Group

What I want to describe and discuss in this chapter is the median group as developed by Pat de Maré. De Maré, who had been part of Foulkes' circle, developed from the year 1974 a unique kind of larger group, which is a transition between the small and the large group. It met regularly for an hour and a half each week as a slow-open group. Its number stabilized at about twenty; the seating was face to face in a circle. I took part in de Maré's group for an academic year, 1983–4. I regard this as my most important group experience, more profound than my small group experiences. I want, therefore, to make an attempt to convey something of my experience of this group: this book would be incomplete without it. What is more, there are many group analysts, group therapists and students of groups who have never heard of the median group.

This chapter is based on my immediate experience of this group: I wrote a paper, 'Experiences in a Median Group', at the time (unpublished, but seen and approved by de Maré). The examples are taken from summaries I wrote after each group meeting. The reader who would like to know more about the subject is referred to de Maré's book on the subject, *Koinonia* (De Maré *et al.* 1991).

The fear of the large group

As de Maré pointed out, Foulkes was sympathetic to the large group, yet it was not until 1972 that the first large group, of more than a hundred members, met with Pat de Maré and Lionel Kreeger as conductors. In 1973 appeared a collection of papers, *The Large Group: Dynamics and Therapy*, edited by Kreeger.

Yet even today there are still many group analysts, and potential group participants, to whom the concept of 'group' is synonymous with 'small group'. The large group to them represents some kind of strange animal, possibly useful for learning purposes but no more than that. Some of the contributors of *The Large Group* have concentrated on the difficulties engendered by it: Turquet (1973) has analysed its threats to identity, while Main (1973) has dealt with processes such as projection and depersonalization and ways of coping with these difficulties. Others have stressed positive aspects of the large group: its potential for being therapeutic in the hospital (Springman 1973) and in the therapeutic community (Whiteley 1973). Hopper and Weyman (1973) analyse the sociology of large groups. De Maré (1973) shows that the large group is particularly suited for fostering and understanding of man in society. He contrasts it with the small group which is psychoanalytic, whereas the large group 'manifests characteristically group-dynamic features.' Many characteristics of 'groups' are thus more evident in large than in small groups. One of these is the emphasis on the horizontal, the here-and-now, as opposed to the vertical, historical approach of psychoanalysis.

I have personally always been fascinated by large groups and rarely experienced the statutory anxiety within them. I have taken part in large groups as participant in a variety of workshops and courses, and as conductor in small therapeutic communities, both a day hospital and a hospital rehabilitation unit. The only large group of which I failed to make sense was the group of 400 strong in the group-analytic congress in Copenhagen, in 1996. The scale and nature of the setting were such that I simply could not hear much of what was said. I cannot therefore say whether I could have integrated the experience had I been able to hear. I fared better in the next very large group, in Budapest in 2000. I must have learnt something in the first group after all.

I found that large groups differ in style from one another, depending on the orientation and personality of the conductor, and of course the members. Some have been sterile exercises in fulfilling a learning task, enlivened only by sparks of humour from group members. A large group, when part of a prescribed course, could become a substrate for complaint and more or less authoritarian rejoinder. When this happens, it becomes a task-oriented group and ceases to have the characteristics of a group-analytic large group.

Other large groups have been fascinating experiences that fostered a process of consolidation, growth and termination within the space of a few days or a few meetings. In a three-day workshop, one conductor (Earl Hopper) showed that metaphor and humour were appropriate currency of interchange in such a group. In another we had, as participants, a very moving experience of togetherness and mourning for losses of war. I cannot recall the identity of the convenor, which means, no doubt, that he or she was a very enabling one. On yet another occasion, in a three-day workshop of large groups only, we worked through experiences of difficulty and conflict on the first day, group dreams and shared meanings on the second day, and mourning on the third day. As chairperson and main organizer I managed to draw all the slings and arrows of the discontented and wondered how to be both an ordinary member and a guardian of boundaries. The conductor (J.

Shakhed, an Israeli living abroad) quickly learnt to become tuned in to local strains and discords and was adept at catalysing the group process. On the third day, he insisted on the reality of death and mourning, exemplified by the death of the group. He thus made it possible for group members to share some very sad personal experiences. For brief workshops, the medium of the large group seems to be ideal in allowing a group process with development and closure, potentially rich in creativity. Small groups in brief workshops can often encourage the start of interpersonal processes which cannot be terminated in so short a space.

The style of conducting a small group is of course important. I was in a small group whose conductor attempted to 'accelerate' interpersonal process by very active interventions, because of the shortness of time, and this proved a boomerang. Conversely, a quietly competent conductor was able to make the small group into a moving experience: this occurred in the small group meeting five times in which I took part in the Copenhagen Congress in 1996. Even the fact that the conductor's erstwhile teacher was a group member did not disturb the balance. This was due to the latter's skill in being an ordinary group member as much as to hers. We began as strangers eager to get to know one another, while aware, almost as soon as we had begun, that we would have to part.

I return to the large group workshop. We have taken, in recent years, to running workshops of a continuous large group, without interim small groups (which were supportive but also diluted and considerably shortened the large group process). It could be two days, preferably three days long. The last one (two days) ended with much enthusiasm and expressions of closeness. My own feeling was that the satisfaction derived from the sense of being part of a larger whole and of being acknowledged as an individual by this whole. From the feedback, it seems that many other participants found it a good experience.

The median group

Anthropological roots

I want, in this chapter, to concentrate on a special kind of larger group developed by P.B. de Maré, the median group. It may surprise some of us to hear that this type of group is rooted in history: it is universal in so-called 'primitive' and long-standing cultures which date back, in some instances, to over 60,000 years ago, coping with the most arduous physical conditions (De Maré 1993). It appears that they meet regularly with no leader and no agenda, making no decisions.

These societies are cooperative rather than competitive, and succeed in abstaining from war, and from major inequalities of wealth and power. We, on the other hand, starve in the midst of plenty, because we mindlessly adhere to an economic subculture which belongs to the age of scarcity, before the invention of the wheel (De Maré 1993).

Development of the contemporary median group

De Maré's median group is a group of a size between the small and the large which has been meeting weekly as a slow-open group, working on group-analytic principles, since 1975. De Maré ran it as a group of about twenty members which could 'slowly expand and grow to a number that has yet to be established.' This number did not constitute a small group, yet was small enough to enable all members to talk to one another. As de Maré points out, it serves as a transition between the small and the large group (personal communication).

De Maré has written his own book, *Koinonia* (with Robin Piper and Sheila Thompson, 1991), on the nature of this unique kind of group. My own involvement is my participation in this group for the duration of an academic year (1983–4). Pat was then taking the group together with Robin Piper as co-therapist, though Robin left before the year ended.

The experience of joining the group in its ninth year

As the group was in its ninth year when I joined, I had no experience of its birth pangs and infancy. A current member who had been there in the first year described it as having been 'cannibalistic'. Page (1978) had described the state of affairs of the group, from a participant's point of view. There was then a good deal of concern with preserving identity. When I joined the group I found little evidence of hate, and preserving identity did not appear to be a problem. I found, at that stage, that the group had a capacity for a good deal of tolerance, concern and caring, which I believe is part of what Pat calls 'koinonia'. When a member was in need, the group would relate to him with infinite patience and great sensitivity, each member contributing in his own individual way, yet acting as part of the group.

As to members' experience of the group, it was important to them, as it was to me. Some said it evoked anxiety, but no one felt a loss or a threat to their identity. It appears (at least to me) that the median group, once established, poses no such threat. Every member is recognized as a person. This is possibly a function of group size, the face-to-face-arrangement in a single circle, but also the mode of conducting the group. In the Tavistock school based on Bion's conception, a large (or even median) group is designed to ignore the individual member. In our median group, four new members joined in the course of the year; they were quickly given recognition as individuals.

Most important, de Maré's median group is continuous over time. A group culture gradually develops and a group memory. Within a few years, the original hate had turned into the impersonal but special kind of friendship Pat designated 'koinonia'.

The group treats the group

The median group is conducted along the principles of group-analytic psycho-therapy, defined by Foulkes (1975, p.3) as 'a form of psychotherapy by the group, of the group, including the conductor'. He stresses that interpretations, conscious and unconscious, are made by patients all the time, other contributions being part associations, part reactions and responses. The conductor should interpret only 'when he has patiently and in vain waited for this insight to come from the group itself' (Foulkes 1975, p.113). Further, the conductor's intervention is called for when there is blockage in communication.

Hence the skill of the conductor consists mainly in making the group the instrument of therapy, enabling it to treat itself. This was very much in evidence in the median group. There was every encouragement for everyone to take on a ther-apeutic function. A 'good' group member might one day bring a personal problem, another day respond to the problems of others. This may be by associa-tion or by recalling similar experiences, by friendly interest or criticism, by analysis or interpretation. Believing that conductors should not be authoritarian, de Maré speaks of 'convenor' rather than 'conductor'. He is, on the other hand, perceived by most members as the father figure of the group. (I have no better expression, though he emphasizes that the median group is not like the family.) This is by no means obvious: I have been in large groups where I found myself surprised when the conductor said something, wondering if he or she had really been on top of things all along.

As de Maré writes in *Perspectives in Group Therapy* (1972), phenomenology can be applied to the conducting of therapeutic groups. He warns that over-interpretation, unnecessary interventions should be avoided. Rather than being 'permissive' and 'accepting' he holds that all contributions are relevant, though we may not always know their meaning. He treated the group as if it had a wisdom and analytic power of its own, and needed to be drawn out rather than supervised and superseded.

In our group, he mostly reserved his interpretations until the group had done its work. Often these were metaperspectives on the group process as a whole. It could be a comment on the present session and its relation to an earlier one. When he focused on individuals, it was usually to encourage those who had not yet spoken or found it difficult to speak or to make themselves heard. His object was to develop the therapeutic powers of the group itself.

Equality and symmetry

Ex. 13(i). Shaun said: 'There is no equality.' Asked what he meant, he replied: 'In the group and outside.' Stephen retorted: 'If you have doubts, it does not make you a worse priest.' Shaun said he did not really have doubts, and the group discussion moved on to charismatic personalities in Christianity, and their claim to love all people equally. Was universal love possible? The group thought not. After a while, I commented that there were charismatic leaders and democratic leaders, ours being of the latter kind. There was indeed equality in the group; what Stephen had meant was that although he might bring himself as a patient, he was still a helping member of the group. (He had, in a recent meeting, occupied the group with problems of his own, quite fruitfully.) Later Stephen said: 'Tonight is the first time the group has given me something.'

This vignette illustrates the equality and symmetry of group members. Equality refers to the egalitarian status of all members, whoever they may be. Symmetry refers to each member's position as both 'patient' and 'therapist' in the group. The conductor is in a position of responsibility, but relies largely on the therapeutic work of the group itself. The conductor's task is to empower the group to be therapist.

Equality of status is a feature of all therapeutic groups. One is an equal member or nothing at all. In professional groups, such as the seminar, or the supervision group, the member competes to be regarded as more knowledgeable, more brilliant than the others. I had once been a member of a seminar in logic in which it was difficult to understand what the tutor was talking about. He would open the class thus: 'Are there any questions? No, then we'll go on.' One week I decided to ask for clarification of the previous week's material. The tutor asked: 'Did anyone not understand? If not, I'll go on.' More than half a dozen students raised their hands. They had, until now, been reluctant to ask. One had to appear knowledgeable.

In the therapeutic group, it becomes clear that there is no hierarchy of 'the more knowledgeable' and 'the less knowledgeable'; competition may occur, but it is not the order of the day. Everyone is equally valued. In the therapeutic dyad, asymmetry is inevitable. As one group member put it, she disliked the thought of individual therapy, because it meant being in a dependent position. In the group, the group member can be both 'patient' and 'therapist', often in the space of the same meeting. This is more obvious in the median than in the small group.

Equality, being on an equal footing, distinguishes the median group from the organization. Organizations typically have a hierarchic structure. The individual in the organization has to compete for a place in the hierarchy. His or her role depends on this.

In the median group, the member's role does not depend on a position in a hierarchy but is based on the member's personality and relationship to the group. (I am using 'role' in the positive sense here, not in the sense of stereotype.)

In the organization, members are all evaluated by a suitable yardstick: qualities such as competence, efficiency, leadership are valued. Role expectations are defined. The development of individuality is not particularly encouraged.

In the median group, there is no yardstick; there is openness of expectation. Hence there is fertile ground for the development of personal qualities, qualities different for each individual. Each member's role in the group is not prescribed and there are no specific expectations. Each person's participation is a function of his or her creativity.

Here is a sequence which illustrates symmetry.

> Ex. 13(ii). When Robin, the co-convenor, announced that he would be leaving, group members asked if anyone would take his place. Pat replied that since no outsider knew enough about larger groups, a co-convenor should be looked for within. A few suggestions were made and dropped. Members asked: 'In what way does a co-convenor differ from an ordinary member?' The group cast about for answers. They recalled the position of Robin before and after he had become a co-convenor. They concluded that a convenor does not talk about himself. They were saying that ordinary members were both therapists and patients. The following week Pat made a suggestion: perhaps members might take it in turns to be convenors. 'Co-convenors?' someone asked. 'No, convenors. Then I will be able to talk about myself.'

Another aspect of equality was that there was no difference in status between those who had come to study group dynamics, and those who had come for personal help. An interesting phenomenon was that it took me months to work out which was which. A family doctor who seemed to be there to learn, to be very much a 'therapist', turned out to be severely depressed. He had been unable to work since his girlfriend was killed in an accident. A psychiatrist who was apparently there to learn nevertheless spoke about fears of hurting his small son. Ultimately, it did not matter: all were in the group to be both 'patients' and 'therapists', both to learn and to be healed and to grow.

Sharing similar experiences

It is a well-known feature of therapeutic groups that they enable the distressed group member to discover that she is not alone in her predicament. Yalom (1981) calls this 'universality', regarding it as one of the therapeutic factors. The median group is a particularly rich field for the potential discovery of shared experience. It is highly likely that there are members who have been in a similar situation, experiencing similar feelings, and others who can illuminate the theme from totally different vantage points.

> Ex. 13(iii). A woman of about 40 talked about a very distressing experience with her mother, expressing a need to be disengaged from her. The following week, the group asked how she was faring. A new member spoke of his dead mother. 'I had loved her, but some years after her death, I found my feelings completely reversed... I don't know why I'm saying this. I've only just come.' Another member said one thought of parents as loving and to be loved, whatever the

reality. He went on to talk about his childhood, which I had never heard him do before.

Individuality

As I have shown in Chapter 5, the therapeutic group is an important instrument in individuation and self-definition. Although at first sight it may seem that 'individual' therapy is more conducive to nurturing individuality, the limitations of any one therapist make for the limitations in outlook, however 'neutral' the therapist may endeavour to be. The wide range of personal differences, even in the small group, makes for a richer palette of possibilities.

In the median group, the range of possibilities is even wider. I sensed this vividly while I was a member of it. Group members had many different lifestyles, and the feeling was engendered that it was all right to be different. The only child of the individual therapist inevitably experiences a yes/no, black/white value system, if only because the therapist has an unconscious value system. In the median group, there is a wide range of colours.

In my notes of those days I wrote:

> The first quality which impressed me about the group was the uniqueness of each individual; the group's accentuation and legitimating of difference. Each member has a unique personality, his own peculiar lifestyle, his own way of perceiving things. A painter said in one meeting: 'People are not interesting unless they get down to what is original about them.' He certainly did so: he would come up with surprising associations, intuitive statements, poetic truths.

I discovered that the opposite of being an individual, of being oneself, was playing a role, becoming a stereotype. As a group member put it: 'The group tries to put you in a role. You have to resist this.' The process is mutual; the group member may fall into a role because it flatters him or suits him and, above all, as a defence against laying bare the real, vulnerable self.

The distinguishing mark of role playing is its predictability. The member who is himself often makes totally unexpected contributions; he is unpredictable and therefore creative and fascinating.

Dialogue

Dialogue in the median group is of a special nature. As one member remarked, it is unlike social dialogue; it has to be learnt. One reason is that social dialogue is usually dyadic, bivalent; the median group dialogue is polyvalent. One must learn to listen, to contribute, to be content to let it pass on. The few members who must repeatedly have the ball back in their court are doomed to frustration, and to being shut up by the group.

De Maré writes of this aspect of the group dialogue. The Platonic dialogue, he points out, was a process of reasoning between two or more people, at most eight; it was different from group dialogue. Arguments are binary oppositions, and basically hierarchical. They are bivalent and digital. Dialogue in the larger group, on the other hand, is polyvalent and analogic. It is egalitarian, 'lateral, tangential, multipersonal' (1991, p.7).

This returns us to a quality I noted about groups in general, and the median group in particular: the potential for a wide spectrum of views, as opposed to the black–white of binary dialogue. We noted its importance in the couples group, where the multicoloured range of views could show the arguing couple that it was not a case of deciding between right and wrong.

In the median group, de Maré sometimes made an interpretation which does not appear in his book on the subject (1991): the theme is sucking and biting, fusion and separation. As infants we suck milk and are unable to talk. We must learn to speak, just as we learn to bite. Biting means hating, but it also means separation and individuation, while sucking means dependence, fusion. Dialogue comes at the end of this process: neither to depend, nor to cut oneself off; to return to others as a consolidated self.

Dialogue in the median group, de Maré points out, transforms hate into koinonia. The very size of the group engenders frustration and therefore hate.

De Maré et al. (1991, p.60) writes that the median group is never at a loss for words; hate is ceaselessly generated. Intuition and experience, however, tell us that dialogue arises not out of hate alone. When koinonia is the prevalent group emotion, there is still fruitful dialogue. Conversely, it would be a mistake to conclude that hate automatically engenders dialogue. In many settings, hate engenders aggression and destruction. It requires a special median group atmosphere for hate to engender dialogue.

In some cases, too, hate precedes the formation of a median group; the latter being set up for the purpose of transforming it. The Black and White Group in London appears to fall into that category. In Israel, the School for Peace has long been running conflict groups for Jews and Palestinians in order to promote under-standing, and therefore transform hate, between the two peoples. The groups are for eight of each people, structured and time-limited, but are in my view akin to median groups. A different kind of mixed group had been conducted by Shafik Masalah with a co-therapist: it was composed of graduate students and had continued for a year (lecture, March 2000). Instead of sharpening conflict, the conductors would ask members for individual meanings of symbols. This would defuse the conflict. I suggest that this was valuable for giving a 'face' to the faceless other.

In Kibbutz Shuval in the Negev, Israel, Kibbutz members have been running combined kindergartens for Bedouin and Kibbutz children since 1992 (Ha'aretz [daily newspaper] 2 August 1998). The Israeli and Bedouin children play together and talk together. Intuition tells us that these children will not hate one another when they grow up. Dialogue, here, will have pre-empted hate.

The inner and the outer

'I find the group unique in showing me various facets of things.' This was said by a rather detached member, when asked what the group meant to him. As de Maré put it, the median group has a great capacity for thinking, for secondary process. It seems to me, however, that primary process is no less important; he who is not in touch with his preconscious cannot work creatively in the group.

As to content, the group dialogue could be concerned either with the inner or the outer world. When dialogue in a small group turns to world problems, this is usually interpreted as a defence or as standing for something else. This is not the case in the median group, which may legitimately talk about social and political concerns.

I would like in this context to mention a lecture given by Earl Hopper in a workshop. Describing an episode in his group, he spoke of a member's description of his childhood environment and the ensuing group discussion. This brought about countertransference imagery of great power. As a result, Hopper made an interpretation which was a turning point in that near-silent group member's participation. This was not a median group, but Hopper regards discussion of society as part of the group process.

Pat used to tell us that the face of the median group is towards society, the larger group outside. It teaches 'outsight' and is rather less concerned with the intrapsychic, with 'insight'.

Nevertheless, I found the group was often free associating very creatively, focusing on the inner world.

> Ex. 13(iv). Leslie, an elderly painter, mentioned a picture in the paper; it was of an old house, which made him feel that time had stood still there. He had had the same feeling in an old church in a village he had once visited. My first association to 'time standing still' was that this safeguarded against 'time running out', a feeling I sometimes experience. However, this could not be true for Leslie; he found 'time standing still' frightening. Now Megan brought a frightening dream from long ago, in which she sent two little boys into a church to get something and they were lost. I asked about their relationship to her. 'One of them is my son.' Pat brought a dream of his. Leslie said he was often taken for a younger man. This for him was negative; inwardly he felt like a child. When admitted to hospital, the doctor asked, did he know he was so high? 'And he was right.' He really had a secret self, a child self, not to be exposed to others. Sheila said surely a lot of people had a secret self. Leslie described his feeling as 'odd man out'. I

brought my own associations: I often felt I was 'odd man out', but I seemed to ask for this, in some ways to cherish it.

I felt that at last I had brought something of myself to the group, made a beginning to being 'treated' by it.

Sometimes there is a struggle whether the theme is inner or outer. At others, one or other dominates. After a group discussing feelings, Pat asked the silent members what they had been thinking. Doreen had thought about the abolition of the Greater London Council, and that she ought to be doing something about it. Martin had been preoccupied with organizational problems connected with his work in housing.

Pat remarked that while the group had focused on the inner world, the silent members had complemented this by thinking of the outer.

On another occasion the reverse process occurred.

Part 3

Ethics and the Group

CHAPTER 14

Towards Ethical Relating

We return to the subject of separateness and belonging. People join groups for a variety of reasons. They emerge from the group process with a better awareness of their identity, of themselves as individuals, as well as a sense of belonging to a larger whole.

The group is there for the individual member, giving something, while the group member has come to understand that she too has responsibilities towards the group, she too has to give to the others.

The benefits of group-analytic therapy evidently extend beyond the actual group, in time and in space. What of the need for giving? Does the group member emerge with a greater awareness of living in a social group, with an enhanced sense of responsibility towards others? There are doubts about the need for ethics in the world today, a world of scientific and technological advances.

One reason is the vague belief that advances in scientific knowledge will solve all problems and increase human happiness. Another is a kind of cynicism; we cannot 'afford' to be moral; in the business as well as in the political sphere, expediency tends to be the dominant ideology. In politics, there is at best a kind of group-egoistic utilitarianism: the outcome (whatever is best for that specific group) justifies the means.

Individualism

Individualism means the right to self-definition and self-determination, the significance of each individual as more than just a member of the social group. The concept is to some extent culture bound; it is relatively modern and associated with Western culture. Individualism is a positive value, yet is often misinterpreted as egoism. However, the right to self-determination does not mean the right to deprive or harm the other.

Some may argue that it is natural and sane to advance one's own interests, even at the expense of others. This is based on a Hobbesian view of humanity: that men compete for scarce resources, even to the point of killing one another; only fear of the law prevents them from doing so. They are willing to submit to a ruler to protect their own life (Hobbes 1968[1651]).

Competitiveness is indeed a common trait in Western culture, evidently a learnt one. Erikson (1950, pp.122–123) describes how a white boy, living in a Sioux community, was perceived as different. The Sioux did not save money and would give away all they had on ceremonial occasions. They called the boy's father 'He-Who-Keeps-His-Money-To-Himself'. White teachers could not get Indian children to compete for excellence, for example in sports (Erikson 1950, p.124). (See also 'Competing and cooperating' in Chapter 4.)

At any rate, we cannot be said, in the twenty-first century, to be living in a world of scarcity. Science has helped us to increase food production. (Unfortunately, some methods of doing this exploit nature, with disregard for ecology and long-term consequences – again, a case of collective egoism.) Famines still occur, but they are the result of wrongful policies rather than of scarcity, as Amartya Sen (1992, p.72) has shown: 'It has been observed that a democracy with a free press tends to eliminate the occurrence of famines through general public pressure on the government to take timely aversive action.' It would seem that we need a group-centred morality: a morality concerned with fairness both within the national group, and within the human group as a whole.

Economics

Capra (1982) criticizes modern economics for being atomistic and reductionist, not seeing the world as a whole and failing to prevent economic crises. There is much poverty in a world of plenty. Economics has embraced the Newtonian model in order to become scientifically respectable. As Capra points out (1982, pp.208–210), competition in the form of 'free market forces' is widely held to bring benefits to all. This is based on Adam Smith's theory that 'the Invisible Hand of the market would guide the individual self-interest of all' (Capra 1982, p.208), producing betterment in the form of material wealth. Capra explains that the model, based on Newtonian physics, makes certain unwarranted assumptions; for example, the instant and complete mobility of all displaced workers, resources and machinery. He also points out that Smith disregarded workers and 'other inferior ranks of people' as well as women. For the model to work, it seems that an exploited and deprived class is needed.

Science alone does not ensure human well-being

There is no doubt that scientific advances bring a great deal of benefit to people. However, little consideration is given to the need for ethical enquiry to guide the application of every new scientific breakthrough. Nuclear energy is an obvious example: a scientific achievement that unleashed a tremendous potential for destruction. Another recent example is genetic engineering. In agriculture, its application has been left to business interests, resulting in irreversible changes which appear to be dangerous to consumers' health and to the ecology.

Poverty and famine are still with us in a world of plenty. Advance in the physical sciences has not ensured human well-being. Nor has progress in means of communications helped us to listen to and understand one another. The science, if there is a science, of how human groups can relate to one another effectively, without being hurtful and destructive, has received little attention. There is violence within and between nation-states, just stopping short of global catastrophe.

However, group therapy and group work organizations have for some time worked on relations between groups. To give one example, the School for Peace in Neveh Shalom, Israel, has developed courses of structured groups for Arabs and Jews, working on inter-group tensions and their resolution.

The 'group culture' of political groups has a very different character from that of therapeutic groups: its morality is based on special pleading, on principles that would never hold up for individuals. Rationalizations are produced to justify injustice: that it is heroic to fight for the interests of one's own group against another. Inhumanity against certain other groups is not inhumanity, since these are defined as sub-human. Political and ideological motivation is held to condone and even glorify acts which would normally be regarded as unethical. It is for the 'cause'; responsibility is assigned to the group. Therefore, everything that benefits the group is allowed. This sounds transparent, put this way: yet the group ethos can be very seductive when the end result is allegedly beneficial to whole groups of people. Consider the long time it took for intellectuals to be disenchanted with communism in practice under Stalin.

The state of our awareness of human relations

Around the year 2000, for all our scientific and technological accomplishments, we are still extremely primitive in human relations, particularly between one social group and another. Large-scale exploitation and violence seems to be rooted in the difficulty of one kind of group to relate to another, to see its members as human beings like themselves. Although there are individuals who are sensitive to the problems of mankind as a whole, many others get caught up in a 'small-group morality' with the features described above. It is therefore clear there is a need for cultivating ethical relating in the modern world.

Human morality and its development

Our questions are these: do human beings have an innate sense of right and wrong? If so, what goes wrong? How does morality develop in the child? Later, we shall consider the role of psychotherapy in the further development of morality and, in particular, that of group-analytic therapy.

The question of human nature: is it moral?

Philosophers have, from time immemorial, asked themselves whether human nature is basically moral. 'The inclination of man is evil from his youth,' (Genesis 8, 21). Is it, indeed? Or is the human infant characterized by 'original innocence'?

Perhaps we should look to psychology for answers. What do we know about the development of human morality? Can anything be done to further it, to increase moral sensitivity?

Consider the question whether we have an innate sense of right and wrong (possibly subject to development). The alternative would be that morality is acquired, inculcated by parents and elders. Since they in turn would have received it from their parents, it would in that case be culture bound. If innate, we may expect common values across cultures. Kohlberg (1971) examined children from different cultures and found that they gave similar answers to questions about moral conundrums. The children were aged 10 to 16 and came from the USA, Mexico, Taiwan, Turkey and Yucatán. This supports the thesis that moral intuitions are innate and universal.

We can distinguish two components in morality: one is based on obedience to authority, and the internalization of that authority. The other is autonomous, based on innate factors; its root is concern for others. Money-Kyrle (1952) describes these two as 'persecutory' and 'depressive' morality: the first is equivalent to the Freudian superego. The second, 'depressive' morality, originates in the Kleinian depressive stage: having in fantasy vented his rage and frustration upon the 'bad' (depriving) breast, the baby comes to realize that the good and bad breast are the same. Out of the baby's remorse arises the need to make reparation.

Since superego values are handed down from parents to children, they are relativistic, different for each culture. Money-Kyrle (1952) points out that the super-ego of a 'good' German Nazi is very different from that of a 'good' British socialist, and is still further removed from that of a 'good' Trobriander or Dobuan. All they have in common is unquestioning obedience.

The second, 'depressive' type of morality is based on loyalty to personal values, compassion and concern. Its owners do not always stand in awe of the law; however, they are more ready to help those in need and take up the cause of the disadvantaged and those who have been wronged.

For Money-Kyrle, moral conflict is conflict between the claims of the two types of conscience when they coexist. Usually one or other type predominates. Money-Kyrle (1952) describes four types of persons: (1) Those who claim to have no moral scruples; this is based on hypomanic denial of conscience. (2) The self-righteous and censorious, whose guilt is 'for export only'. In types (3) and (4), there is consciousness of conscience. Type (3) is the authoritarian type, obedient to a severe superego or to an external authority. In (4) the depressive element predominates. This type is concerned more with loyalty to his own values than with authority; he is unafraid of disobedience.

Another name given by Money-Kyrle to the 'depressive' conscience is the 'humanist' conscience.

Piaget (1932), in his research of the development of morality in children, found that there were two developmental phases. In the first, derived from parental authority, the child follows commands, but is unable to give reasons for what she does. Piaget called this 'heteronymous morality' or 'morality of duty'. In the second phase, beginning from ages 7 to 12, the child develops an egalitarian morality. Some situations present conflict between obedience and solidarity: for example, when a father asks a child to tell him if her brother has behaved badly. With increasing age, solidarity becomes stronger than obedience (Piaget 1932, p.289). Piaget (1932, p.293) states: 'Egalitarian justice develops with age at the expense of submission to adult authority and in correlation with solidarity between children.' Piaget (1932, p.317) stresses that egalitarian justice develops through living together and that its essential feature is reciprocity.

It seems that the child also learns to respect and consider the other, to understand that the other has feelings as she does, since we find that she initiates acts of kindness and generosity which are in no way prescribed. Piaget called this phase 'autonomous morality' or 'morality of love'.

It is not difficult to see that Piaget's 'morality of duty' closely corresponds to Money-Kyrle's 'superego' morality, while Piaget's 'morality of love' or 'autonomous morality' closely corresponds to Money-Kyrle's 'depressive' morality (Chazan 1979).

Like Money-Kyrle, Piaget describes different types of adult character: 'There are even individuals…to whom goodness matters far more than duty, and the converse is also true' (Piaget 1932, p.352).

The difference between the two is that Money-Kyrle presumes 'depressive morality' to arise in infancy, while Piaget traces its development to the peer group stage. It may be that there is no contradiction, that the foundations for autonomous morality are laid in infancy, while further development occurs through association with the peer group at a later stage.

Psychoanalytic perspectives on morality

The dominant view in psychoanalysis has been to regard the field of morality as outside its concern. While Freud considered 'the ability to love' as one of the criteria of mental health, he believed it was impossible to love one's neighbour as oneself. He tended to regard beneficent traits as reaction formation, generosity as reaction formation against stinginess. Hartman (1962), however, held that psychoanalysis should not be regarded as liberating man from morality. Zilboorg (1951) pointed out that not all sense of guilt is neurotic. He recalls the apocryphal story of the man who consulted Freud because he was unhappy, while leading a rather free sex life. 'You don't need psychoanalysis,' said Freud, 'what you need are a few good inhibitions.'

The view of Wilhelm Reich is interesting.

> The healthy person has no compulsive morality; he has no impulses which call for moral inhibitions… Sadistic fantasies disappear…to rape a sexual partner becomes inconceivable, as do ideas of seducing children…in brief, all the phenomena point to the fact that the organism is capable of self-regulation. (Reich 1969, pp.6–7)

Clearly, Reich believed that the healthy id is moral; the superego is not needed here. He concentrated, however, on sexual morality alone.

Fromm, Suzuki and de Martino (1960) point out that humans must adapt to society to avoid collision; this is an ego function and not part of morality. In order to survive, every society has to exploit the majority. The majority accepts this voluntarily, its conscious mind being filled with suitable fictions. Similarly, the nature of repressed material is culture dependent. A man in a peaceful tribe would repress a wish to kill, while one in a warlike tribe would repress a revulsion against killing (perhaps feeling nausea instead). Thus, the unconscious may contain moral as well as anti-moral wishes. Its discovery in therapy can be enriching, both enhancing morality and making people more free to be themselves. (cf. Chazan 1997).

As we have seen, Money-Kyrle (1952) is interested in morality and describes a theory of moral development. As to psychoanalytic treatment, he argues that it helps to free the individual from irrational persecutory anxieties, thus making for movement away from the authoritarian type of conscience towards the humanist one.

Charny (1996, 1997) is a psychotherapist who diagnoses evil as a sickness. He calls for a category of 'Personality disorder of excessive power strivings' (1997, pp.3–15). Charny (1996, p.478) suggests 'a definition of evil as doing harm to human life', classifying mental health diagnoses into the above, versus the traditional disorders of functioning of the self. In the same paper, he enlarges on family members doing harm to others and on the difficulties of treating these in an individual framework. Mittwoch (1987) holds that the therapist ought to make the patient aware of guilt of which he is unaware, for example to help him realize that he has hurt another person.

In their study of families, Boszormenyi-Nagy and Spark (1984) find tacit accounting of obligation, repayment and entitlement, ranging over two or three generations. One might express the sense of entitlement thus: 'I cannot take anything for myself unless I also give to others in the family.' He would probably conclude that excessive giving, too, is unhealthy. The mother who can only give, is unwilling to receive, whose child cannot make a difference to her, is likely to engender a sense of impotence and futility in her child. In Boszormenyi-Nagy and Spark's view the essence of therapeutic work consists of revealing this tacit accounting and distinguishing healthy and reciprocal from pathological and exploitative forms of relating.

Is there a place for morality in psychotherapy?

Psychotherapists tend to believe that the patient's morality is not their concern. The underlying rationale is that the therapist must be neutral; she ought not to moralize. She must not be authoritarian or directive.

However, being human, therapists can hardly be neutral. Nina Coltart holds that:

> we are, whether we like it or not, conveying moral judgments in many of the things we say...it seems to me that not, at least to acknowledge this is to be imprisoned within a straitjacket of denial or to turn a blind eye to important aspects of ourselves, and to what we may be imposing on our patients. (quoted in Berke et al. 1995, p.167)

We should, moreover, distinguish between 'morality' and 'moralizing'. 'Moralizing' implies an authoritarian stance, being didactic on ethical issues in the patient's life. It is analogous to taking on a superego function. Making possible the development of 'morality', on the other hand, does not mean telling our patients what to do, what is right and wrong. It involves the cultivation of specific inner qualities. It may mean developing their sensitivity to the feelings and needs of others, their awareness of the nature of their own way of relating to their fellow-men.

Virtue theory and psychotherapy

We are helped here by developments in ethical theory. Moral theories concern themselves either with the act, with its consequences, or with the agent. Utilitarian theories focus on consequences, whereas deontological theories focus on the act itself. Thus, a deontologist would say that lying is always wrong, while a utilitarian might at times justify it if the consequences of telling the truth were worse. A third possibility is to focus on the qualities of the agent. This is the rationale of virtue ethics, a relatively young theory which, however, has its roots in Aristotle. Stetman (1997, p.11) points to some of the implications of utilitarian theory: for the best outcome, it may be indicated to betray a friend. As to deontological theory, with its emphasis on duties, 'it is surely possible, and indeed often the case, that people who violate no duty nevertheless behave in an inhumane and disgusting manner' (Stetman 1997, p.7). According to virtue theory, we act beneficently because we want to be that sort of person. We help a friend because she is our friend, not because it is a 'duty' or because it is expedient.

In virtue ethics, bonds between persons are valued above duties and utilities:

> If we made the justificatory principles of these theories into our motives, the result would be destructive to the moral life and to the relationships between human beings. No friendship would exist if we helped our friends merely 'out of duty', or because we thought that such help was needed for the maximization of happiness. (Stetman 1997, p.6)

In virtue ethics, we are interested in character; its 'primary object of evaluation is persons or inner traits of persons rather than acts' (Zagzelski 1996, p.15).

A virtue theory of morality seems to be the appropriate one for psychoanalytic psychotherapists. Virtue ethics is not interested in duties, which means the therapist is not tempted to tell the patient what he ought to do. The focus is on character traits, on 'inner traits of persons'.

Areas of morality: the interpersonal and the group

Let us consider the areas in which morality operates. For our purposes, the main areas of relevance are two: one is interpersonal relating, the other is justice and fairness within the social group. (There are others, such as relationship to animals, to nature, to future generations, but these do not concern us at present.)

There is also the important but difficult area of relationships within the large group, i.e. humanity as a whole; this involves relationships between groups. As already mentioned, there is increasing awareness of deprivation and injustice, even cruelty to other national groups, done by deed or by omission, though it may be difficult to devise strategies which might prevent or reverse these. Our large group sense of justice is still in its infancy.

Interpersonal relationships

By interpersonal we basically mean two-person relationships, though the threesome may come into it. Good interpersonal relating means more than behaving justly or doing one's duty. It depends largely on our ability to understand and empathize with the other, to put ourselves in her shoes.

The basis of relating well to the other is the recognition of the other as a person in his own right: in object-relations language, as a whole object and not a

part object. Another way of expressing this is in Buber's (1937) 'I–Thou' terminology: to recognize the other as a person ('I–Thou') rather than a figure in a
transaction ('I–It'). The other is not merely playing a role, fulfilling a function for
us; he is subject to recognition as a person, sensitive, vulnerable like ourselves.

Intra-group relating

The second area, relationships with the group, is based mainly on a sense of justice
and fairness. One model is that of Kant (1948, p.70): we are asked to consider
what would happen if everyone did what we did; to behave, as he phrases it, in a
way that could become universal law. Another aspect is the issue of fair shares. A
philosopher who has worked out a theory of fairness, based on our moral
intuitions, is John Rawls (*A Theory of Justice*, 1972). Rawls stresses the importance
of justice as fairness, as against utilitarianism, where the sum total of utilities
matters rather than fair distribution. This means that some individuals may be
seriously disadvantaged; in fact, the individual tends to disappear in utilitarian
theory, both as recipient and as agent. As a model for fairness, Rawls uses the
device of 'the veil of ignorance', suggesting that we divide the cake as if we were
ignorant of which slice would be ours.

Basic principles of group and two-person relationships

The sense of justice and fairness can be expressed by Kant's principle 'always act
in such a way that your action could be a universal law' (1948, p.70). On interpersonal relations, he held that we must 'always treat the other as an end in himself,
never as a means to an end' (1948, p.95). This is a way of saying that the other
should be treated as a person in his own right.

We can go further than Kant, however, in the ethics of interpersonal relating.
For one thing, Kant did not favour empathy or reciprocity as a means. He listed
codes of duty, and considered it moral only if one visited the sick out of duty,
rather than from any sense of empathy with his suffering – or because one loved
the person. (This results in logical difficulties, as loving persons would lead to the
agent being less moral than he would be if he did not love.) Kant's ideas on this go
as far as rationality takes us. However, we have additional means for guiding our
relationship with the other: 'we have direct, immediate, non-sensory knowledge
from within…inner experience can be so varied and many-sided, complex and
difficult to understand, and profound in its implications and significance, as outer
experience'. This was written by a philosopher, Schopenhauer (Magee 1997). It
seems to be a good definition of empathy: knowing the other through looking
within, by analogy with self-knowledge.

Let me digress by saying that this is an ability which most of us possess, some
to a greater degree than others. High-grade autistics, suffering from Asperger's

syndrome, cannot experience emotions and cannot therefore imagine them in others. They have to learn, intellectually, what is expected of them. Less extremely, some types of persons are relatively ungifted in the field of human relations. My husband and I once visited an acquaintance we had not met since we were in our early twenties, he being slightly younger than us. He was now a grammarian. Talking of old times, whenever we mentioned a mutual friend, our host brought the conversation back to grammar. It seemed that human relations were outside his field of expertise. Not surprisingly, he never married.

As to philosophical theories of morality, most fail to emphasize the role of empathy and reciprocity, of putting oneself in the other's place and acting accordingly. Of moral psychologists, Kohlberg (1971) speaks of true reciprocity in stage 6, the highest stage, the stage of universal ethical principle. We have to distinguish this from stage 2, instrumentalist-relativist orientation, also described as 'you scratch my back, I'll scratch yours'. In stage 6, the individual understands the other and imagines how the other must feel. Hence he does to the other as he would want to be done by.

A moral philosopher who assigned importance to empathy, or something related to it, was Iris Murdoch (*The Sovereignty of Good*, 1970). She wrote of 'attention' as a basis or moral relating. By an act of imagination we can 'really see' the other as a person, and cease to regard him as the object of our own needs. She gave the example of a woman who regards her daughter-in-law as vulgar. Could she 'look again' and perhaps see her differently?

Murdoch held that our actions begin with our perception of persons or things. 'Willing' an act therefore begins long before it is time to act. We can see that her philosophy was in harmony with psychotherapeutic thinking, where the work is on the perception of self and others.

Moral development and the group-analytic group

Let us now consider the role of the group in moral development. It is not far-fetched to consider it analogous to the childhood peer group, and the analogy extends to the peer group function of furthering moral development. The therapeutic dyad is usually regarded as analogous to the parent–child relationship. The respective roles of therapist and patient, as well as the transference and countertransference, make it so. This is the basic nature of the relationship, although ideally the therapist does his best to be unbiased, open and enabling. (The morality of a patient who has been in individual therapy might be compared to that of an only child whose parent has done her best to be enabling, permissive and empowering.)

Do we have clinical evidence that the group furthers the moral development of the group member? Foulkes believed that it did. Foulkes and Anthony (1957, p.74) describe the development of communication patterns in the small group.

A.B., aged 30, male; single; complains of incapacitating shyness in company and feelings of inadequacy.

Analysis of first week sample showed majority of communications directed towards conductor with high coefficient of egocentricity. Statements refer to his symptoms and feelings towards them, and feelings as a result of them. Looks bored and detached when other members are bringing up their problems.

Second analysis six months later. About 40% of communications now group-directed. Increase in 'mirror reaction' and in interpretative and sympathetic responses. Some tendency to sub-grouping. Marked increase in use of 'we' and 'us'.

Third analysis six months later. About 40% communications now group-directed. 'Mirror' and 'chain' responses now very much in evidence. Increase in altruistic responses. (Has joined social club connected with his job. No dependency reactions.) (Foulkes and Anthony 1957, p.74)

Foulkes and Anthony (1957) seem to take it as understood that diminution in egocentricity, and increased ability to listen to and respond to others, and to the group as a whole, are part of the growth of a group, and part of the process through which group members go. In other words, there is moral progress.

Among Foulkesian group analysts who consider the role of the group in moral development, Dennis Brown is prominent. In his lecture given at the 'Sib-Links' workshop in 1995, he discusses sibling rivalry and the role of the group in helping members move on to a sense of fairness and justice (Brown 1998a).

Later Brown (1998b) writes at length of the role of the group-analytic group in developing the sense of justice. If we wonder how the group, despite members' psychopathology, can recognize what is just, we are referred to Foulkes' Basic Law of Group dynamics (Brown 1998b, p.392; Foulkes 1948, p.29): 'Together they constitute the norm from which, individually, they deviate.' Brown, however, also emphasizes the role of the conductor 'as a Monitor of Justice' (1998b, p.403) and in his impartiality, 'recognizing everyone's equal value' (Brown 1998b, p.405). Brown holds that the therapeutic group is indeed analogous to the peer group in moral training: 'To paraphrase Foulkes: it's a form of peer-relationship training-in-action' (Brown 1998b, p.406) (cf. Chazan 1993a).

Let us consider the role of the group in furthering growth in the main areas of morality: (1) interpersonal relating, (2) justice and fairness within the group and (3) fairness between groups.

Interpersonal relating

The group is an excellent medium for arriving at mutual respect and recognition, for understanding one another. The group member may find that another is 'like him' in some respects, but also finds many differences and learns to understand

and respect others. Often he may find himself empathizing with another and at times attempting to put himself in the other's place. This surely increases sensitivity to others and provides the basis for better interpersonal relationships in life, and for more ethical relating between persons. In Iris Murdoch's (1970) language, the group member will have had practice in 'really seeing' the other.

It has to be said that in our daily life we deal with many persons as representatives of their function – the bank clerk, the supermarket cashier, and so on. There is no time or space to give attention to them as persons. They have, as Hopper and Weyman (1973, pp.168–169) point out, roles which are specific, while good teachers, close family members and friends have 'diffuse roles'. What about the group member? The unstructured nature of the therapeutic group makes a member's role diffuse, which makes for anxiety, but makes it possible to see his or her humanity.

The importance of specific roles is illustrated by a film which caricatures encounter groups. In the film, some group members go out to lunch and proceed to assign a diffuse role to the waiter, asking about his life and generally relating in a way which the waiter finds embarrassing.

Justice and fairness within the group

How do group members acquire a sense of justice and fairness in the group? I suggest that they go through a learning process, not entirely conscious, much as a childhood peer group does. If it were spelt out, what is learnt is something like 'what would happen if everyone behaved as I did'. For example, some group members do not immediately understand the importance of attending regularly. They expect, however, the group to be there for them when they do attend. Slowly they come to understand that if everyone did as they did there would be no group. When I conducted a couples group which at one stage consisted of only four couples, any couple who was unable to attend would contact all the others to make sure there would be sufficient (i.e. three couples) to make a group. If not, they would let me know.

The shared assumption tends to be that each group member deserves a reasonable share of group time and energy. However, it is usually understood that a particularly needy member deserves, at least temporarily, more time and attention. Needy group members sometimes exploit the group's generosity, consciously or otherwise.

Ex. 14(i). A woman known to be in distress came to a meeting, giving the group to understand that she could not talk, but felt very troubled. She held the group in a spell for a long time, with everyone wanting to enable her to speak, and not daring to bring up their own, seemingly lesser problems. I believe that there was an element of enjoyment in the power she wielded over the group.

On the other hand, a group member who never takes anything for himself may wrong not only himself but also the group, by causing concern and guilt feelings.

> Ex. 14(ii). In a group of outpatients who had been psychotic, Peter was troubled by many problems. He was an intelligent and well-educated divorced man with a child he had not seen for years. He had obsessional traits, and a low frustration tolerance. The group had witnessed his angry impatience when he had to wait to speak, or wait for an answer. The group knew that there were difficulties in his relations with his parents (though he lived alone). Yet there were whole sessions when Peter did not make use of the group. Not only the therapists were concerned about this; the group expressed concern, in part blaming themselves and expressing some guilt feelings.

There are group members who take on the role of adviser, good Samaritan and guru.

> Ex. 14(iii). In a group of post-psychotic and borderline outpatients, Daniel seemed stronger than other members. (He had, in fact, never been treated in hospital.) He would relate with kindness to others and often give advice. The group liked this and put him in the role of guru. It is difficult to know how much the fulfilment of this role was at the expense of getting help for himself. Daniel married while he was in therapy in the group, and then began to talk about his own problems, though not often. He remained, however, the person who could be relied on to have a kind word for a group member in distress. It was clear that he understood others and empathized with them.

> On one occasion, Aaron opened the session by telling the group he had fallen at night, apparently fainting. His family doctor had found nothing wrong. The group knew that Aaron lived alone and that his family had ignored him since his mother's death. He had often spoken of his loneliness. David said: 'I think you fainted because you felt that nobody needed you.'

This was as good an interpretation as anyone could have made.

Group members may ask for help for themselves but must also listen to others and contribute their help. Conversely, it is understood, usually, that to be constantly the Good Samaritan is not enough; one must also be willing to expose one's own weakness, to be able to ask for help, to see the need for change in oneself.

On the whole, we learn from clinical observation that group members go through a process of moral learning. They learn to respect one another as individuals, learn what makes the group 'work' and seems just and right within it. This seems to be analogous, on the one hand, to the growth, in the peer group, of consideration and love for other individuals, different from themselves but no less vulnerable; on the other hand, to the process of a peer group of children learning what makes a game work and what makes for fairness to all its members.

Brown (1998b, p.403) emphasizes the role of the group conductor as 'monitor of justice'. 'This might include apologizing for our own mistakes.' This latter is important in emphasizing reciprocity between the conductor and the group, that the conductor, too, obeys the laws and is no dictator. In my view, however, the group should not and need not depend on the conductor's monitoring. It seems preferable, and more in the spirit of Foulkes, to empower group members to look for the principles of justice themselves, which they are well able to do.

Personally, I find it difficult even to be a good role model. Mostly, it is not difficult to carry out the conductor's task of righting the balance when required: for example, to direct the group's attention back to a distressed member whose communication was cut short or who was unable to make his voice heard at all. At other times it seems impossible to decide justly between competing claims, and it is probably best to let the group decide, to let the group process take its course.

If we consider the analogy of the childhood peer group, according to Piaget, we recall that egalitarian justice develops through association with the group, often in opposition to the commands of parental or authority figures. This is good reason to empower the group to work out principles of justice for themselves.

Fairness between groups

This area is problematic and, as yet, relatively unexplored. It is suited to work in median and larger groups.

Sibling rivalry and its resolution

Sibling rivalry does of course play a part in the group, in the form of competition for the conductor's attention. On the other hand, moral learning in the group is much more than resolution of this rivalry. There are issues other than being the conductor's favourite child. Just as the childhood peer group discovers, unaided by any parent or authority figure, the rules of egalitarian justice, so can the group-analytic group. The role of the conductor is to play down his or her own importance, to lessen the group's dependence, and facilitate the group's work towards justice and fairness.

The sense of fairness within family and group

Boszormenyi-Nagy, a family therapist, has shown how the sense of fairness operates as a backbone of relationships within the family group. He uses the concept of 'entitlement', expressed thus: 'I cannot take anything for myself unless I also give to others in the family' (Boszormenyi-Nagy and Spark 1984). This could very well be applied to the therapy group: 'I cannot take anything for myself unless I also give to others in the group.' In the course of the group process, group members come to feel this intuitively: they do not feel 'entitled' to receive the attention of others unless they have related attentively to others in the group.

Brown uses the term 'entitlement' in a different sense, as a 'personal affirmation of rights', or, as 'a pathological claim for special privileges...based on deep-seated narcissistic wounds', illustrating with examples from group sessions (Brown 1998b, pp.403–404). In my view, however, Boszormenyi-Nagy's usage very aptly fits an aspect of the sense of fairness, as a moral quality, which could also be developed in the group-analytic group.

> Ex. 14(iv). In an outpatient group of post-psychotic and borderline patients, Aaron would often demand the group's attention for a large part of the session. When the group had devoted some thirty minutes to his problems and moved on to someone else, he would protest vehemently. 'You are not taking any notice of me. I am going to set fire to myself.' He was like an infant whose needs required immediate satisfaction, who did not feel he existed unless he was the centre of attention.
>
> After working in the group for some time – and in the case of such a group this means years – Aaron changed. He had learnt to listen to others and to relate to their preoccupations. He clearly understood that if he did this, he too could expect the group's attention when he needed it. He had developed a 'sense of entitlement', in Boszormenyi-Nagy's sense.

Dennis Brown, in his usage of 'entitlement', might argue that Aaron had moved from this to developing a sense of justice. I suggest, however, that he had moved from an infantile sense of 'I am entitled to all I need' to earning his entitlement, at least within the group, and that this was an intuitive and largely unconscious learning process.

Between self and other

The group is the place par excellence in which a group member can develop the capacity to perceive the other as a person. Whether he sees parts of himself in the other, or sees him as completely different, it is possible to put himself in the other's position and understand how he feels. The group situation is both more open and more securely bounded than a social situation can be. As group member, one has permission to explore the life story and feelings of the other, without fear of being regarded as curious. The price is the obligation to respond with one's whole self. At the same time, any obligations incurred by extending sympathy and help are bounded by the time and space of the group.

Moral rules and 'rules of the game'

An objection might be raised that what is learnt in the group are not principles of morality but 'rules of the game'.

Ex. 14(v). In one small group of neurotics, a professional man expressed concern. He had been in the group for a year but did not feel he had benefited. Another group member suggested he could have made better use of the group. He had been very helpful to others but never spoken of his own problems. 'It is true, I do not think I ever learnt the rules of the game.'

This illustrates the point, though somewhat tangentially. There are those who see living in society in terms of 'keeping the rules of the game'. Our professional would speak of 'investing' in a person to gain a friendship.

I suggest that there are, indeed, 'rules of the game', and that they are specific to a school of group therapy. The group begins when the conductor closes the door. The group lasts for a specific period of time and is terminated by the conductor. The group member should attend regularly and, if he cannot, notify the group of his absence. These are not moral rules, they are 'traffic rules' that serve to preserve the group situation.

Ex. 14(vi). In the team meetings in an Arbours Community, one guest/patient had a need to leave, recurrently, the room in which the team meeting took place (Berke *et al.* 1995, p.74). His therapists understood this was his way of reassuring himself that he could come and go, that he was not trapped. His going in and out was accepted, though in many groups it might have been against the rules of the game. (This was not the usual kind of therapeutic group, but one consisting of one 'guest' and several therapists.)

There are also 'rules of the game' which are specific to a particular group, part of the group culture which has developed unconsciously in the course of its history.

Ex. 14(vii). In an experiential group workshop for professionals, the constant refrain was: 'Talk for yourself, do not talk about what is happening in the group.' The group was apparently intolerant of professionals acting as 'therapists' rather than 'patients', persons who revealed themselves, in the group. In another workshop for professionals, there seemed to be no such rule. Members were free to talk about either themselves or about what they perceived as happening in the group. The rules of the game were different.

We see that 'rules of the game' seem to be specific to group psychotherapy, or to a particular school of thought, or to the culture of a specific group. Moral rules, on the other hand, are universal.

The peer group of children learn to play a game in a way that works, discovering their own rules on the way. They also learn to treat one another fairly. The rules of each game may be idiosyncratic, but the rules of fair behaviour general and remain part of the child's character. In the same way, rules of fair behaviour are discovered in the therapeutic group, becoming part of the group member's personality.

Small groups and median groups

The small group reflects the family, and any relationship which is smaller than its own size: the dyad, the triad, and so on. Sibling rivalry can be experienced in it, and reflect sibling rivalry in life. Jealousy of a twosome, experienced by a third person, is reflected in group relations. Relating to a father or mother figure, in whatever form, is observable mainly in transference to the therapist. One way this differs from transference manifestations in dyadic therapy is its openness to observation by the whole group.

A larger group has the capacity to reflect larger relationships. The median group reflects society. Within it, there are more possibilities than in the small group. The group is still small enough to enable relating between two members. It can also reflect the relationship between groups. In one median group meeting, the issue of homosexuality arose. The group was able to discuss the plight and problems of homosexual couples as compared to heterosexual ones.

On other occasions it discussed the difficulties of the lone wolf in being gregarious.

The median group, by its nature, holds the possibility of promoting understanding of other ways of thinking, other ways of living. We could be talking about dyadic relating: just as a group member could understand and empathize with another who was in a different life situation or felt differently about things, he could understand an individual who belonged to a different ethnic or ideological or national group.

On the other hand, the median and the large group can model relationships between groups, be they ethnic, religious, national, or whatever.

Since median groups are useful for working out relations between groups, they may be deliberately composed of members of groups in conflict. In London, there is a Black and White Group. In Israel, work has been done on groups of Jews and Palestinians in the School for Peace in Neveh Shalom and in other settings. These were structured and time-limited groups, but there seems to be no reason why similar problems could not be worked out in unstructured and ongoing groups. This is a field that invites further work.

Beyond dealing with specific cultural issues, intercultural tensions, the median group has a civilizing effect on society. This might sound fantastic to some, yet is supported by anthropological evidence, cited by de Maré (1994). So-called primitive societies, such as Aborigines, Inuit and Dogrib Indians, hold meetings of 20–40 persons, with no agenda and no leader. These societies succeed in being cooperative and not competitive, avoiding war and inequalities, and using natural resources without exploitation thus surviving in difficult conditions. There is evidence that these date back some 60,000 years. We, on the other hand, 'starve in the midst of plenty' (de Maré 1994, p.203), for all our intellectual, scientific and technological sophistication. We seem powerless to organize society to our mutual benefit, to refrain from exploitation of and cruelty to sectors of society. The absence of large and median group dialogue in society, may well be connected with this. (See also Chapter 12.)

Summary

The group-analytic group appears to be a medium in which moral growth can take place. Group members develop their moral sensitivity and their autonomous morality in the course of the group process. Growth occurs in at least two areas: first, in the area of interpersonal relating, through the development of understanding and empathy with others, at times going on to reversibility: the ability to put oneself in the other's shoes and not doing to others as one would not be done by. Second, in the area of intra-group relating, by members discovering for themselves what makes a group, any human group, work and what is justice and fairness within it. It is probable that this can be generalized to life outside the group.

There is a third area, that of relationships between groups and within the large group of humanity as a whole. Although we know less about this, it is likely that the large group, and particularly the ongoing median group furthers development of this capacity. This is an area which requires further exploration.

References

Ackerman, N.W. (1961) *The Psychodynamics of Family Life: Diagnosis and Treatment of Family Relationships*. New York: Basic Books.

Agazarian, Y. and Janoff, S. (1993) 'Systems Theory and Small Groups.' In H.I. Kaplan and B.J. Sadock (eds) *Comprehensive Group Psychotherapy, Second Edition*. Baltimore, MD: Williams and Wilkins.

Alexander, F. and French, T.M. (1946) *Psychoanalytic Therapy*. New York: Ronald Press.

Andrews, J. (1998) 'R.D. Laing in Scotland: Facts and Fictions of the "Rumpus Room" and Interpersonal Psychiatry.' In M. Grijswijt-Hofstra and R. Porter (eds) *Cultures of Psychiatry*. Amsterdam: Atlanta.

Balint, M. (1969) *The Basic Fault: Therapeutic Aspects of Regression*. London: Tavistock.

Barcai, A. (1967) 'An Adventure in Multiple Family Therapy.' *Family Process 6*, 185–192.

Barham, P. (1998) 'From the Asylum to the Community: The Mental Patient in Postwar Britain.' In M. Grijswijt-Hofstra and R. Porter (eds) *Cultures of Psychiatry and Mental Care in Postwar Britain and the Netherlands*. Atlanta, GA: Rodopi.

Barker, P. (1991) *Regeneration*. London: Viking.

Barnes, M. and Berke, J. (1971) *Two Accounts of a Journey through Madness*. London: MacGibbon and Kee.

Baron, C. (1987) *Asylum to Anarchy*. London: Free Association Press.

Bateson, G. (1972[1935]) 'Culture Contact and Schismogenesis.' In *Steps to an Ecology of Mind*. New York: Chandler.

Bateson, G. (1972[1964]) 'The Logical Categories of Learning and Communication.' In *Steps to an Ecology of Mind*. New York: Chandler.

Bateson, G. (1979) *Mind and Nature: A Necessary Unity*. New York: Bantam.

Bateson, G., Jackson, D.D., Haley, J. and Weakland, J. (1956) 'Towards a Theory of Schizophrenia.' *Behavioral Science 1*, 251.

Benedict, R. (1936) *Patterns of Culture*. New York: Penguin.

Berke, J., Masoliver, C. and Ryan, T.J. (1995) *Sanctuary: The Arbours Experience of Alternative Community Care*. New York: Process Press.

Bion, W.R. (1952) 'Group Dynamics: A Review.' *International Journal of Psychoanalysis 33*, 235–247.

Bion, W.R. (1961) *Experiences in Groups*. London: Tavistock.

Bloch, S. and Crouch, E. (1985) *Therapeutic Factors in Group Psychotherapy*. Oxford: Oxford University Press.

Boscolo, L., Cecchin, G., Hoffman, L. and Penn, P. (1987) *Milan Systemic Therapy*. New York: Basic Books.

Boszormenyi-Nagy, I. and Spark, G.M. (1984) *Invisible Loyalties: Reciprocity in Intergenerational Family Therapy*. New York: Brunner-Mazel.

Bott, E. (1976) 'From Hospital to Society.' *British Journal of Medical Psychology 49*, 97–140.

Bowen, M. (1964) 'Family Relations in Schizophrenia.' In A. Auerbach (ed) *Schizophrenia*. New York: Ronald Press.

Bowen, M. (1976) *Family Therapy in Clinical Practice*. Gardner Press.

Brown, D. (1998a) 'Fair Shares and Mutual Concern: The Role of Sibling Relationships.' *Group Analysis 31*, 3, 315–326.

Brown, D. (1998b) 'Foulkes' Basic Law of Group Dynamics 50 Years on: Abnormality, Injustice and the Renewal of Ethics.' *Group Analysis 31*, 4, 391–419.

Buber, M. (1937) *I and Thou*. Trans. R.G. Smith. Edinburgh: T. and T. Clark.

Capra, F. (1982) *The Turning Point: Science, Society and the Rising Culture*. London: Fontana.

Charny, I.V. (1992) *Existential Dialectical Marital Therapy: Breaking the Secret Code of Marriage*. New York, NY: Brunner Mazel.

Charny, I.V. (1996) 'Evil in Human Personality. Disorders of Doing Harm to Others in Family Relationships.' In F.W. Kaslow (ed) *Handbook of Relational Diagnosis and Dysfunctional Family Patterns*. New York: Wiley and Sons.

Charny, I.V. (1997) 'A Personality Disorder of Excessive Power Strivings.' *Israel Journal of Psychiatry 34*, 1, 3–15.

Chazan, R. (1979) 'The Conscience in Psychological Theory and Therapy.' *Israel Annals of Psychiatry and Related Disciplines 13*, 3, 189–200.

Chazan, R. (1984) 'Experiences in a Median Group.' Unpublished paper.

Chazan, R. (1993a) 'Moral Growth in the Group Analytic Group.' Unpublished paper.

Chazan, R. (1993b) 'Group Analytic Therapy with Schizophrenic Outpatients.' *Group 17*, 3, 164–178.

Chazan, R. (1997) 'The Patient as Moral Agent in Psychotherapy.' *Israel Journal of Psychiatry 34*, 1, 26–36.

Chazan, R. (1999) 'The Group as Therapist for Borderline and Psychotic Patients.' In V.L. Schermer and M. Pines (eds) *Group Psychotherapy of the Psychoses*. London: Jessica Kingsley Publishers.

Chazan, R., Levi-Posnanski, A. and Tal, A. (1989) 'From Dependence to Autonomy: Dilemmas in the Development of a Therapeutic Community in a Psychiatric Hospital.' *International Journal of Therapeutic Communities 10*, 4, 8–20.

Clark, D.H. (1974) *Social Therapy in Psychiatry*. Harmondsworth: Penguin.

Clark, D.H. (1996) *The Story of a Mental Hospital: Fulbourn 1858–1983*. London: Process Press.

Coltart, N. (1995) 'Attention.' In Berke, S. Masoliver, C..and Ryan, T.J. (eds) *Sanctuary: The Arbours Experience of Alternative Community Care*. New York, NY: Process Press.

Copeland, B.J. and Proudfoot, D. (1999) 'Alan Turing's Forgotten Ideas in Computer Science.' *Scientific American* April, 99–103.

Curry, A.E. (1965) 'Therapeutic Management of Multiple Family Groups.' *International Journal of Group Psychotherapy 15*, 90–96.

Dalal, F. (1995) 'Conductor Interventions: To "Do" or to "Be"?' *Group Analysis 28*, 379–393.

Davidson, S. (1993) *Holding on to Humanity – The Message of Holocaust Survivors: The Shamai Davidson Papers*. Ed. I.V. Charny, with the editorial assistance of D. Fromer. A publication of the Institute on the Holocaust and Genocide, Jerusalem. New York and London: New York University Press.

Davies, I., Ellenson, G. and Young, R. (1966) 'Therapy in a Group of Families in a Psychiatric Day Centre.' *American Journal of Orthopsychiatry 36*, 134–146.

de Maré, P. (1972) *Perspectives in Group Psychotherapy: A Theoretical Background*. London: George Allen and Unwin.

de Maré, P. (1973) 'The Politics of the Large Group.' In L. Kreeger (ed) *The Large Group: Dynamics and Therapy*. London: Maresfield Reprints.

de Maré, P. (1984) Personal Communication.

de Maré, P. (1994) 'The Median Group and the Psyche.' In D. Brown and L. Zinkin (eds) *The Psyche and the Social World*. London: Routledge.

de Maré, P., Piper, R. and Thompson, S. (1991) *Koinonia: From Hate through Dialogue to Culture in the Large Group*. London and New York: Karnac.

de Waal, F. (1996) *Good Natured: The Origins of Right and Wrong in Human and Other Animals*. Cambridge, MA: Harvard University Press.

Durkheim, E. (1952) *Suicide: A Study in Sociology*. Trans. J.A. Spandy and G. Simpson. London: Routledge and Kegan Paul.

Durkin, J.E. (ed) (1981) *Living Groups: Group Psychotherapy and General Systems Theory*. New York: Brunner-Mazel.

Erikson, E.H. (1950) *Childhood and Society*. New York: Norton.

Ezriel, H. (1973) 'Psychoanalytic Group Therapy.' In L.R. Wolberg and E.K. Schwartz (eds) *Group Therapy: An Overview*. New York: International Books.

Foulkes, S.H. (1948) *Introduction to Group-Analytic Therapy. Studies in the Social Integration of Individuals and Groups*. London: William Heinemann Medical.

Foulkes, S.H. (1964) *Therapeutic Group Analysis*. London: George Allen and Unwin.

Foulkes, S.H. (1975) *Group Analytic Psychotherapy*. London: Maresfield Library.

Foulkes, S.H. and Anthony, E.A. (1957) *Group Psychotherapy: The Psychoanalytic Approach*. Harmondsworth: Pelican.

Frankena, W.K. (1973) *Ethics*. Englewood Cliffs, NJ: Prentice-Hall.

Freud, S. (1921) 'Group Psychology and the Analysis of the Ego.' *The Standard Edition of the Works of Sigmond Freud, Volume XI*, 193–208.

Freud, S. (1924) *A General Introduction to Psychoanalysis*. New York: Washington Square Press.

Fromm, E. (1978) *To Have and to Be*. London: Jonathan Cape.

Fromm, E., Suzuki, D.T. and De Martino, R. (1960) *Zen Buddhism and Psychoanalysis*. Norwich: Souvenir Press.

Gelcer, E., McCabe, A.E. and Smith-Resnick, C. (1990) *The Milan Family Therapy: Variant and Invariant Methods*. Northvale, NJ and London: Jason Aronson.

Gombrich, E.H. (1968) *Art and Illusion*. London: Phaidon.

Guntrip, H. (1968) *Schizoid Phenomena, Object Relations and the Self*. London: Hogarth Press.

Hartman, H. (1962) 'Psychoanalysis and Moral Values.' The Freud Anniversary Lecture Series. New York: IUP.

Hegel, F. (1910) *Phenomenology of Mind*. London: MacMillan.

Heimann, P. (1950) 'On Countertransference.' *International Journal of Psychoanalysis 31*, 81–84.

Hes, J. and Handler, S. (1961) 'Multidimensional Group Psychotherapy.' *Archives of General Psychiatry 5*, 92–97.

Hinshelwood, R.D. (1999) 'How Foulkesian was Bion?' *Group Analysis 32*, 4, 469–484.

Hobbes, T. (1968[1651]) *Leviathan*. Harmondsworth: Penguin.

Holton, G. (1973) *Thematic Origins of Scientific Thought*. Cambridge, MA: Harvard University Press.

Hopper, E. and Weyman, A. (1973) 'A Sociological View of Large Groups.' In L. Kreeger (ed) *The Large Group: Dynamics and Therapy*. London: Maresfield Reprints.

Jones, M. (1968) *Social Psychiatry in Practice. The Idea of the Therapeutic Community*. Harmondsworth: Pelican.

Kanas, N. (1993) 'Group Psychotherapy with Schizophrenics.' In H.I. Kaplan and B.J. Sadock (eds) *Comprehensive Group Psychotherapy*. Baltimore, MD: Williams and Wilkins.

Kanas, N. (1999) 'Group Psychotherapy with Schizophrenic and Bipolar Patients: Integrative Approaches.' In V.L. Schermer and M. Pines (eds) *Group Psychotherapy of the Psychoses*. London: Jessica Kingsley Publishers.

Kant, I., (1948) *Groundwork of the Metaphysics of Morals*. Trans. H.J. Parks. London: Hutchinson.

Kennard, D. (1998) *Introduction to Therapeutic Communities*. London: Jessica Kingsley Publishers.

Kohlberg, L. (1971) 'From Is to Ought: How to Commit the Naturalistic Fallacy and Get Away With It in the Study of Moral Development.' In T. Mischel (ed) *Cognitive Development and Epistemology.* London and New York: Academic Press.

Kreeger, L. (ed) (1973) *The Large Group: Dynamics and Therapy.* London: Maresfield Reprints.

Kreeger, L. (1991) 'The Psychotic Patient.' In J. Roberts and M. Pines (eds) *The Practice of Group Analysis.* London: Routledge.

Kymissis, P. (1993) 'Group Psychotherapy with Adolescents.' In H.L. Kaplan and B.J. Sadock (eds) *Comprehensive Group Psychotherpy.* Baltimore, MD: Williams and Wilkins.

Laing, R.D. (1960) *The Divided Self.* London: Tavistock.

Laing, R.D. (1961) *The Self and Others.* London: Tavistock.

Laing, R.D. (1985) *Wisdom, Madness and Folly.* London: Macmillan.

Laing, R.D. and Esterson, A. (1964) *Sanity, Madness and the Family.* Harmondsworth: Penguin.

Laing, R.D., Phillipson, H. and Lee, D.R. (1965) *Interpersonal Perception.* London: Tavistock.

Laqueur, H.P., Le Bart, H.A. and Morong, E. (1964) 'Family and Group Therapy.' *Current Psychiatric Therapies IV, V.*

Lefevre, D.C. (1994) 'The Power of Countertransference in Groups for the Severely Mentally Ill.' *Group Analysis 27,* 441–447.

Lefevre, D.C. (1999) 'Psychotherapy Training for Nurses as Part of a Group Psychotherapy Project: The Pivotal Role of Countertransference.' In V.L. Schermer and M. Pines (eds) *Group Psychotherapy of the Psychoses.* London: Jessica Kingsley Publishers.

Leichter, R. and Shulman, G.L. (1966) 'Emerging Phenomena in Multi-Family Group Treatment.' *International Journal of Group Psychotherapy 18,* 59–69.

Levin, E.C. (1966) 'The Multiple Family Therapy Group.' *International Journal of Group Psychotherapy 18,* 59–69.

Magee, B. (1997) *Confessions of a Philosopher. A Journey through Western Philosophy.* New York: Random House.

Main, T.F. (1946) 'The Hospital as Therapeutic Institution.' *Bulletin of the Menninger Clinic 10,* 66–70.

Martin, D.V. (1962) *Adventure in Psychiatry.* Oxford: Bruno Cassirer.

Masalah, S. (2000) 'The Social Unconscious in Action.' Lecture to Israel Society of Group Psychotherapy.

Matte Blanco, I. (1975) *The Unconscious as Infinite Sets: An Essay in Bi-Logic.* London: Duckworth.

Mazor, A., Gampel, Y. and Horwitz, G. (1992) Interviewers' Reactions to Holocaust Survivors' Testimony. *Echoes of the Holocaust,* Israel.

Mittwoch, A. (1987) 'Aspects of Guilt and Shame in Psychiatry.' *Group Analysis 20,* 33–42.

Money-Kyrle, R. (1952) 'Psychoanalysis and Ethics.' *International Journal of Psychoanalysis 33,* 225–234.

Mullan, H. and Rosenbaum, M. (1973) *Group Psychotherapy, Theory and Practice,* 2nd edn. New York: The Free Press.

Murdoch, I. (1970) *The Sovereignty of Good.* London: Routledge and Kegan Paul.

Page, P. (1978) 'The Large Group 1977.' *Group Analysis 11,* 34–39.

Piaget, J. (1932) *The Moral Judgment of the Child.* Trans. M. Gabain. London: Kegan Paul, Trench, Trubner.

Pincus, L. (1976) *Death and the Family: The Importance of Mourning.* New York: Vintage Books.

Pines, M. (1998) 'Reflections on Mirroring.' In M. Pines. *Circular Reflections: Selected Papers on Group Analysis and Psychoanalysis.* London: Jessica Kingsley Publishers.

Pullen, G. (1999) 'The Therapeutic Community and Schizophrenia.' In V.L. Schermer and M. Pines (eds) *Group Psychotherapy with the Psychoses.* London: Jessica Kingsley Publishers.

Racker, H. (1968) *Transference and Countertransference.* London: Hogarth Press.

Rapoport, R. (1960) *Community as Doctor.* London: Tavistock.

Rawls, J. (1972) *A Theory of Justice.* Oxford: Oxford University Press.

Reich, W. (1969) *The Sexual Revolution.* New York: Farrer, Strauss and Giroux.

Resnick, S. (1999) 'A Biography of Psychosis: Individuals, Groups and Institutions.' In V.L. Schermer and M. Pines (eds) *Group Psychotherapy of the Psychoses.* London: Jessica Kingsley Publishers.

Ruesch, J. and Bateson, G. (1951) *Communication: The Social Matrix of Psychiatry.* New York: Norton.

Rycroft, C. (1966) *Anxiety and Neurosis.* Harmondsworth: Penguin.

Rycroft, C. (1979) *The Innocence of Dreams.* London: Hogarth Press.

Rycroft, C. (1995) *A Critical Dictionary of Psychoanalysis, Second Edition.* Harmondsworth: Penguin.

Sacks, O. (1995) *An Anthropologist on Mars.* London: Picador.

Salzberg, H.C. (1962) 'Effects of Silence and Redirection of Verbal Responses in Group Psychotherapy.' *Psychological Reports 11*, 455–461.

Sandison, R. (1998) 'Memory and Psychotherapy: Individual and Group.' *Group Analysis 31*, 53–70.

Schafer, R. (1982) *The Analytic Attitude.* Worcester MA: Basic Books.

Schermer, V. and Pines, M. (eds) (1999) *Group Psychotherapy of the Psychoses.* London: Jessica Kingsley Publishers.

Schneider, S. (1999) 'Resistance, Empathy and Interpretation with Psychotic Patients.' In V. Schermer and M. Pines (eds) *Group Psychotherapy of the Psychoses.* London: Jessica Kingsley Publishers.

Searles, H.F. (1965) *Collected Papers on Schizophrenia and Related Subjects.* New York: International Universities Press.

Searles, H.F. (1979) *Countertransference and Related Subjects.* New York: International Universities Press.

Sen, A. (1992) *Inequality Re-examined.* Oxford: Clarendon Press.

Sere, I.B. (1995) 'Rites of Passage.' In Berke, J., Masoliver, C. and Ryan, J. (eds) *Sanctuary and the Arbours Experience of Alternative Community Care.* New York, NY: Process Press.

Simmel, G. (1950) *The Sociology of Georg Simmel.* Glencoe, IL: Free Press.

Singer, P. (1983) *Hegel.* Oxford: Oxford University Press.

Skynner, R. (1976) *One Flesh, Separate Persons: Principles of Family and Marital Psychotherapy.* London: Constable.

Skynner, R. and Cleese, J. (1993) *Life and How to Survive It.* London: Methuen.

Sprott, W.J.H. (1958) *Human Groups: A Study of How Men and Women Behave in the Family, the Village, and Many Other Forms of Association.* London: Penguin.

Stetman, D. (ed) (1997) *Virtue Ethics.* Edinburgh: Edinburgh University Press.

Swogger, G. (1981) 'Human Communication and Group Experience.' In J.E. Durkin (ed) *Living Groups: Group Psychotherapy and General Systems Theory.* New York: Brunner Mazel.

Turquet, P. (1973) 'Threats to Identity in the Large Group.' In L. Kreeger (ed) *The Large Group: Dynamics and Therapy.* London: Maresfield Reprints.

Urlic, I. (1999) 'The Therapist: Role in the Group Treatment of Psychotic Patients and Outpatients.' In V. Schermer and M. Pines (eds) (1999) *Group Psychotherapy of the Psychoses.* London: Jessica Kingsley Publishers.

Van Bertalanffy, L. (1966) 'General System Theory and Psychiatry.' In S. Arieti (ed) *American Handbook of Psychiatry.* New York: Basic Books.

Van Bertalanffy, L. (1968) *General System Theory.* New York: George Braziller, Inc.

Walzer, M. (1998) *Spheres of Justice.* Oxford: Martin Robertson.

West, M. (1963) *The Shoes of the Fisherman.* London:Pan Books.

Whiteley, J.S. (1973) 'The Large Group as a Medium for Sociotherapy.' In L. Kreeger (ed) *The Large Group: Dynamics and Therapy.* London: Maresfield Reprints.

Whiteley, J.S. (1999) 'Attachment Theory and Milieu Therapy.' *Group Analytic Contexts 14,* 24–27.

Yalom, I. (1980) *Existential Psychotherapy.* New York: Basic Books.

Yalom, I. (1981) *Group Psychotherapy: Theory and Practice.* New York: Basic Books.

Zagzelski, L.T. (1996) *An Inquiry into the Nature of Virtue and the Ethical Foundations of Knowledge.* Cambridge: Cambridge University Press.

Zilboorg, G. (1951) *Sigmund Freud.* New York: Charles Scribner.

Zinkin, L. (1983) 'Malignant Mirroring.' *Group Analysis 16,* 2, 113–126.

Zinkin, L. (1997) Personal Communication.

Subject Index

acceptance 56–8
administrator, dynamic 41
analyst,
  interpreting 28
  observing 28
anxieties, staff 145–6
asylum 138

belonging 51–2,56–9, 177

causality 40
causation
  horizontal 17–18
  circular 35
cohesiveness 44,45,58
communalism 130
communication 103–4
community, therapeutic 129–148
  for long-stay patients 141–8
complementarity 53–4
concern 70
concordance 66
conflict theory
  in couple 154–5
conformity 52–3
containment 138
co-therapy 119–20
countertransference 88–9, 99
  with chronic schizophrenics 142,143
couples therapy 23
creativity 92,93
custody 138

defenses 121
  in couples group 155–6
democratization 130
dependency 90
depersonalization 164
determinism 34,40
dialogue

in median group 170
dimensions
  in couples group 149–50
  in family group 117–9
  in therapeutic community 129
discordance 66, 129
discussion, free-floating 108
double bind 114
dyad, therapeutic 28

economics 178
effectiveness (personal) 143
entropy 34
environment
  producing chronicity 141–2,148
equality 167–9
equifinality 34,40
existential aspects 109–112
expression of emotion, difficulty in 23–4

factors, therapeutic 103–7
fantasy 28–9
feeling understood 67
flexibility 62–3
free-floating discussion 37
function (of group)
  facilitating 123–128
  mutative 123–129
fusion/separation 171

group,
  couples 149–161
  group-centred 101–2
  inner 44,46
  interpretations by 75
  large 48, 63–5, 91, 147, 163–5
  in primitive cultures 165
  leader-centred 101–2
  median 49, 68, 163, 165–175
  multiple family therapy 113–128
  slow-open 98
  stability of 45
group culture 45
  of political group 179
group process

Author Index